Make It Rain

Rain

Ten Tried-and-True Imperatives
for Small Business Success

Leonard Fischer, ESQ

Leonard Fischer
Benetrends, Inc.
1684 S Broad St, Suite 130
Landsdale, PA 19446

Paperback ISBN: 978-0-9993523-2-8
Hardback ISBN: 978-1-7371960-0-6

This book is memoir. It reflects the author's present recollections of experiences over time. The author has attempted to recreate events, locales, and conversations from memories. Because memories cannot always be reliable (especially when an author has had more than 80 trips around the sun), some names and characteristics have been changed, some events have been compressed, and some dialogue has been recreated. In order to maintain their anonymity, in some cases names of individuals or places have been changed or omitted, as well as characteristics and details such as physical properties, occupations, places of residence or places of business.

Although the author and publisher have made every effort to ensure that the information in this book was correct at press time, the author and publisher do not assume and hereby disclaim any liability to any party for any loss, damage, or disruption caused by errors or omissions, whether such errors or omissions result from negligence, accident, or any other cause.

Benetrends, Inc. is a Retirement Plan Services Provider and their employees do not provide legal or tax advice. You may not rely on the information contained in this book for such purposes and should consult your independent legal and/or tax advisors. Benetrends, Inc. is not an investment advisor and does not represent or sell investments or securities of any kind.

Printed in the United States of America

*This book is dedicated to Cheryl…and to
everyone who helped the two of
us build our dream.*

*And to you, the new business owner,
I hope it helps you achieve your own dreams
of financial independence.*

You begin by always expecting good things to happen.

— Tom Hopkins

Contents

Dear Reader:

If you've made it here, I can only assume you're in one of the most exciting states of the human condition: you're thinking about opening your own business. Decades ago, I was where you are right now. And I can tell you, unequivocally, that business ownership is the most empowering, life-changing move you can make for yourself.

Still, if you're anything like the thousands of employees we've helped to become entrepreneurs, and right now you're experiencing some combination of wonder and worry, you're in luck. I wrote this book for you.

- If you feel stuck or disillusioned in the role of employee, manager, or corporate executive despite the fact that you've "succeeded,"

- If you're frustrated, feel constrained or locked in a box, are following orders from people who know less than you, and are not being paid what you feel you deserve,

- If you're longing for a different way—a way toward personal and financial freedom that leads to true wealth and the lifestyle of your dreams,

- If you're a "wantrepreneur"—excited by the idea of running your own show, but put off by the perceived risks or complications associated with it,

- If you're not quite retirement age but are still worried that time is running out and your entrepreneurial ship has sailed,

- If you sometimes wonder whether you've got what it takes—and self-esteem struggles keep you from pursuing your deepest desires, this book is for you.

Over the coming pages, I want to share with you the most powerful secret I know: you don't need special powers, the "right" personality, or an MBA to enjoy the personal freedom that business ownership provides.

My name is Leonard Fischer, and I have none of those "secret weapons" for business. I'm an ordinary guy who grew up in a low-income section of Brooklyn sleeping on a pull-out couch with my brother.

I was an awkward, introverted kid who was often picked last in gym class and was underestimated most of my life. A below-average student without a competitive bone in my body.

Yet when I was nearly 50 and down to my last dollar, I designed a retirement planning product that transforms employees into entrepreneurs and launched a twenty-million-dollar business. That same product spawned an industry that launched tens of thousands of new small businesses. Against all odds, I created a lifestyle for myself and my family beyond my wildest imaginings, and facilitated the American dream for countless others in the process.

Believe me when I tell you it wasn't magic, it wasn't genius, and it wasn't special training that determined my trajectory in the second half of life. It was simply a willingness to take a chance on myself and a relentless commitment to remaining positive, curious, and determined to go back for more…even on the toughest of days. Running a business requires an enthusiasm for problem solving and the humility to admit you don't have all the answers. A business is essentially a series of unexpected obstacles that are placed in your way, day after day.

The entrepreneurs who create dream lives for themselves are open to learning and not afraid to ask for help. Over the past 30 years, I've asked for help more times than I can count. And now I want to help you. In the coming chapters, I'll show you how to "make it rain" in the form of profits for you and your family.

Becoming wealthy while working for someone else can often be a long-term uphill battle. After all, an employee's income and benefits are a corporation's expenses. And more often than not, the goal is to keep those expenses to a minimum.

But when you open a business and fund a retirement plan in the process, you can design your own benefits package as your ticket to freedom and wealth. The Rainmaker Plan® and Rainmaker Advantage Plan® were created precisely for that purpose, and you'll find a full explanation of both programs later in this book.

If you take nothing else away from this book, I hope you'll appreciate that the financial system in America was built to favor business owners. And that once you understand the rules, you can be the kind of business owner who builds a future for yourself beyond your wildest imaginings.

From the heart,
Len

PRELUDE

The Binding Contract You Never Meant To Sign

Before I jump into the delicious meat and potatoes of business ownership, I want to address a common American myth.

One of the things I hear most often about small business ownership—and I hear it from clients, accountants, attorneys, and investment brokers—is that it's risky. I suspect you hear that too. Folks say there's more stability in an old-fashioned j-o-b than in running your own company. And while that may have been the case many moons ago, I cheerfully beg to differ with the crowd. (And I do so from my beautiful seaside home on Coronado Island with a 50-foot sailboat docked right outside.)

The "social contract" between employer and employee has a complicated history dating back to the industrial revolution. You see, before that, most folks were farmers or entirely self-sufficient in some way. As America became industrialized, companies needed workers. But they didn't have a way to lure them away from their homes into jobs that were difficult, and sometimes dangerous. So they created perks, the most common of which was a pension.

According to the US Railroad Retirement Board, the first industrial pension plan in America was created by a railroad company in 1874. The implied contract between the company and its employees was something like, "You work for us, and we'll take care of you when you're done."

The problem with that contract, and most others like it, is that it wasn't regulated in any way. And these companies that created pensions made it awfully hard for their workers to collect. In fact, there were so many hoops to jump through, few workers ever received benefits.

In 1913, the Sixteenth Amendment to the Constitution was ratified, granting Congress the power to tax personal income. At the same time, a system was set up to collect taxes at the source, as they're collected today. Pension plans became tax-deductible, which was a boon for corporations. So guess what happened? That's right. They became more popular than ever. And as unions sprung up around the country, negotiations for pension plans at big organizations became pretty common. But the folks working for little companies were left out, and the government eventually created Social Security to encourage older workers to step aside for younger ones to take their place.

After World War II, pension plans were at the height of their popularity. But there was still no regulation of these plans, and abuses by employers ran rampant. That is, until 1963, when the Studebaker company underfunded its pension plan and more than ten thousand employees who believed they'd be taken care of in their retirement were left out in the cold, with no recourse. In 1974, the Employee Retirement Income Security Act (ERISA) was passed to protect employees from pension fraud and abuse.[1]

Guess what happened when pensions became regulated? Fewer and fewer companies offered them. And by the '80s, 401(k)s had surpassed pension plans, and employees began socking away money to plan for their own futures.

At one point, 88% of American workers had pension plans.[2] Today only 21% of Americans participate in pension plans.[3] And employers aren't even inclined to match 401(k) funds any more. Big corporations—and even the US government—have stripped away retirement benefits little by little in order to cut costs. And the contract that started between employers and employees during the industrial revolution has turned completely upside down. Now it is the employees who are securing the future for corporations. Oddly, though, the belief that being a lifelong employee is the most "secure" way to plan for the future is still valid.

You may be reading this and thinking a pension plan isn't so important. That you need a job primarily for the benefits, like health insurance or paid vacation or generous sick leave. But sadly the contract on those advantages has run out in America as well. As of January 2021, less than half of American workers get their health insurance from their employer. And depending on which political party runs the show (and which industries lobby the hardest), the reliability of that number fluctuates wildly.

What's more, every state in the US has at-will employment. Which means that unless you're in a state with rare exceptions that are covered by a written contract (there are 14 of those), your employer can fire you at any time with no notice and no reason, and you can't sue.[4] Beyond that, your salary is taxable and your tax deductions are severely limited. The tax laws in America favor your employer. And believe me, they're getting the better end of the deal.

The truth is, employment is an iffy situation. If you had a great contract attorney, I bet they'd tell you not to sign a contract that would give your employer none of the obligations and all the perks. Yet Americans still live under the impression that they're secure and taken care of if they have jobs.

My experience over the past four decades has led me to believe the opposite is actually true. Americans are best taken care of when they're self-reliant as business owners. According to *The Millionaire Next Door* by William Danko and Thomas Stanley:

> *Twenty percent of the affluent households in America are headed by retirees. Of the remaining 80 percent, more than two-thirds are headed by self-employed owners*

of businesses. In America, fewer than one in five households, or about 18 percent, is headed by a self-employed business owner or professional. But these self-employed people are four times more likely to be millionaires than those who work for others.[5]

When you own a business, you design your own benefits plan. You determine what your retirement will look like. You negotiate your pay plan with yourself. You build your healthcare benefits into your business plan, along with your paid vacation and sick leave. You benefit from deductions associated with allowable perks. You control the future of the company…and the future of your life.

So if you're putting off this decision because it feels risky, I invite you to consider this question:

Who would you rather rely on to secure your well-being? You or your employer?

Over the next 11 chapters, I'm going to lay out for you the benefits of business ownership, and my personal imperatives for running a business well. And at the end, you can ask yourself that question again. I won't ask you to take my word for it—only that you hear me out and then decide for yourself. Read on to learn about my first imperative and where to begin.

Imperative #1:
Don't Be Afraid To Start In The Middle

I was 44 when I found myself in the very position you may be in as you read this book—starting over. To put it bluntly, I was starting from nothing.

On the day the first half of my life ended and the second half began, I found myself aimlessly wandering through a parking lot with fewer than 50 spaces, searching hopelessly for my car. In a sweat-soaked suit and soggy tie, I trudged lap after lap in the scorching California midday sun, straight past my car each time.

I couldn't see it. Because every bit of my attention was squarely focused on the shame that gripped my chest and the fear that had sunk like a boulder to the pit of my stomach. Both were reactions to the bankruptcy petition I'd just signed in my attorney's strip-mall office. The moment was surreal.

I have no memory of driving out of the parking lot that day. But I do recall stopping at the store to buy some food for dinner. At the checkout, I stood dazed and shaken until I heard a persistent beep. "Sir, your card was declined. Do you have a different one?" There I stood, slack-jawed and red-faced in front of the cashier, halfway through life with nothing material to show for it, wondering how I'd ever recover. It remains one of the most sobering moments of my existence.

The journey to that humbling spot was relatively unremarkable. I'd moved from Pennsylvania to California after a painful divorce, and purchased an automotive tune-up franchise from an owner looking for an exit strategy. I'd already had some luck with a transmission store, and this seemed like a well-aligned venture.

At the time, I was a skilled pension attorney but a naïve and inexperienced entrepreneur. So when I'd purchased the business, it was lost on me that the seller had cooked the books. More specifically, he'd paid his employees off-the-record so the business appeared to be profitable, but actually wasn't. As you can imagine, I didn't get very far when I brought in my own team. The employee expenses outstripped the revenue in embarrassingly short order. And I bled cash trying to keep it open longer than I should have.

You might think the lesson of this story is that you should do your homework before purchasing a business. But while that's sage advice, it's not nearly as critical as the gold nugget I hope you'll mine from my experience.

To finish wealthy and happy, start in the middle. "The middle of what?" you might ask. The middle of life.

What I didn't know then that I understand now is that midlife is the perfect time to make your move. I learned this from my own evolution, and from assisting thousands of people who started again at 40, 50, and beyond.

Adlai Stevenson said, "What a man knows at 50 that he did not know at 20 is, for the most part, incommunicable."[6] And I couldn't agree more. By midlife, you've mastered skills and acquired knowledge that make you better at all kinds of things, running a small business included.

If you're considering open a business mid-life, you've likely stockpiled some funds for retirement as well. And if you're anything like me and the rest of the midlife business owners I've met, you developed a certain wisdom and resilience during the first half of life that, when applied to the second half, will make success a whole lot more feasible.

So if you're concerned that you're late to the party, set that worry aside. It's never too late to take control of your destiny.

You might also find some comfort in knowing that many people who open businesses in the middle of life feel terrified. And lost. So if you're suffering from a case of the jitters, you should know that you're in good company.

Why is the middle of life the prime time to start a business? Read on to learn about the most common reasons.

No more wise guys/gals.

My experience with midlife—and with my clients who've hit it—is that we're not quite the wise guys and gals we were when we were younger. By the time we hit 40 or 50, we're more willing to admit that we don't know everything, because we have less to prove. And because leadership that is compassionate and humble—and therefore effective—is more about listening than anything else, it literally pays to open your ears.

And I don't know about you, but I was more willing to receive and incorporate feedback at 50 than I was at 25. And I'm even more ready to hear and value it today, at 80.

You can afford to take a risk and have some fun.

When we're raising kids, the stakes are different. Not necessarily higher, just different. When you're providing for a family, reliable sustainable income is a blessing. It makes everything simpler. But once your kids grow up and leave (and if they haven't yet, I promise they will), it's common for your risk tolerance to grow.

I sometimes hear people say that 50 or 60 is too late to start over and put your savings on the line. But I know firsthand, and I've seen it time and again with clients—you'll have more time, attention, wisdom, and energy to give to a business now than you ever had before. And when the day-to-day pressures of parenting are removed, you're free to make choices you'd likely have avoided earlier on.

Plus, if you've saved for retirement, you can afford to take a risk. Because there's always time to begin again. And if you start a business doing something you love to do, you won't want to retire. (Take it from me—I'm 80 and writing this book!)

You've earned it.

In the first half of life, we pay our dues. It may sound trite, but it's true. We study, learn, take the lousy shifts, strive and grind to make progress, and allow our ambition to rule our pace and commitments. So by the time you're ready to leave the 9 to 5 and start your own thing, you've earned the right to enjoy yourself, and you've invested enough in your own development to benefit from the payoffs.

Don't get me wrong—opening and running a business is hard work. But it's *your* hard work. And if you set it up correctly, the business is designed to serve you and your lifestyle and desires, rather than you serving someone else's. If you've paid your dues, why not reap the rewards?

Experience through osmosis.

Simply by walking the earth for four, five, or six decades, you've mastered all kinds of skills. You've likely learned to multitask and negotiate to get what you want. You're wiser to the ways of the world and make more discerning decisions. You've prob-ably had a 25- or 30-year career where you participated in a business environment and managed or influenced others or par-ticipated on a team. You've learned valu-able lessons about money, and even more about people. Because of all of this, you're wise. And wisdom breeds confidence.

I love to see folks choosing entrepreneur-ship in midlife because they're better sea-soned for what's required from a business owner: patience, self-assurance, cool-headedness, humility, judgment, resil-ience, and the willingness to slow down and do things the right way.

Regret is a powerful motivator.

When people look back on their lives, it isn't the fact that they've failed at something that really bothers them. It's that they never tried.

In the middle of life, we begin to see the possibilities of regret. And we come to understand that if we don't make moves now, we may never make them. A willingness to try and fail drove me to some of my most profitable and rewarding decisions. And I've found that the fear of regret is a much more convincing argument for change than the fear of not getting it right.

You've likely surmised by now that after that afternoon of aimless wandering in the bankruptcy attorney's parking lot I picked myself up and soldiered on. I decided to turn back to what I knew best, and I hung out my shingle as a pension attorney. I rented a tiny office a distance from downtown inside an existing law firm. My space was so small that my assistant worked out of the conference room. And every time my landlords held a client meeting, my assistant had to skedaddle.

And while my office space was meager and my ego was slightly battered, it was inside those offices—and inside that hungry, blank-slated space of beginning again—that I launched Benetrends. It was from virtually nothing that I dug deep and found the ingenuity and creativity to design an entirely new product to catapult employees into entrepreneurship. A product so novel and so useful that it would spark the growth of an entire industry and become the catalyst to launch tens of thousands of new small businesses.

And it was not in spite of the fact that I'd lived nearly 50 years of my life by then, but precisely *because* of it that I was persistent, resourceful, and wise enough to pull it off.

Imperative #2:
Be Smart...
But Not Too Smart

In those early days at Mission Brewery Plaza, I put my head down and built a real business. Before I created The Rainmaker Plan I developed an excellent reputation for designing pension plans for big firms. I sold the plans through Guardian Life Insurance, and I was a big producer for them. I did so well for Guardian, in fact, that they gave me the funds to move out of that other law firm's office and into Benetrends' first official corporate headquarters.

The pipeline for new business was good. And it was reliable. One of the most solid investments I made during that time was sales training for myself. It turned me from an introverted policy wonk into a confident talker who relished the sales game. And before too long, I was reeling in big fish, day in and day out. I even built my way up to a staff of 16 employees.

So you might consider it shocking (I know I did) that I found myself wandering aimlessly once again—this time through the paisley-carpeted aisles of a retirement industry convention—with that old familiar vice grip of shame in my chest as I stared down the possibility of yet another bankruptcy. I hadn't signed on the dotted line just yet. And I was searching desperately for a way to avoid it. All 16 of those employees I'd hired were gone. And so was my own monthly income.

You see, even though I was consistently landing new clients, Benetrends wasn't turning a profit. Because those big fish would invariably swim away. The trouble was, I spent all of my time on the front end designing the plans. I was comfortable there in my own expertise. But pension plans need more than just solid design. They're complicated financial instruments that require administration, compliance, and financial reporting. And I'd spent little time or energy building the processes or the teams required to support those functions. Benetrends was downright lousy at them.

As clients left in frustration, instead of solving what was really a pretty mundane systems issue, I leaned further into my expertise and brought in more big fish. And when the going really got rough, I supplemented my income doing work as a bankruptcy attorney. Oh, the irony! Month after month, money walked in through the front door and snuck straight out the back.

I ended up wandering the aisles of that industry convention because I'd failed to follow one of the cardinal rules of small business:

It pays to be just smart enough.

As it turns out, being an expert in the law or pension plan design is not the same as being an expert business owner or leader. And this is important for you to understand, because chances are that you're coming from a career where, like me, you developed mastery. I'll bet you came from an environment where you were required to be the smartest you could be in any given moment. An environment where innovation and ingenuity won the day.

But as an owner, you'll find that some aspects of your business won't benefit from creativity or stellar vision. You'll need systems—reliable, repeatable, measurable, teachable systems. If you're too smart, you may skip, ignore, or override proven systems or fail to see a simple solution that already exists. And in this way, the most sensational businesses can fail in the most routine and com-monplace ways.

It was that kind of failure I was experiencing when I headed out to that conference. And you know what I found? Outsourcing companies. Loads of them. Entire entities designed to make plan administration not only simple, but also consistent and reliable.

And directly from the trade show booth of one of those firms, I recruited my first management-level employee. It was an investment in the ordinary. A commitment to the routine, tedious, everyday side of the business that I loathed but knew I couldn't live without. It was a smart choice for me. Just smart enough.

Being just smart enough means more than just acknowledging systems. It means joyfully main-taining a beginner's mindset. It means approach-ing your business with a sense of wonder and curiosity. If you already know all the answers, or you're too smart to be a beginner, you miss out on the brilliance that's available to you in every moment. Here are some specific ways you can do this effectively.

Listen more than you talk.

I often tell my employees (especially the sales team) that we were born with two ears and one mouth for a reason: to listen twice as much as we talk. No one knows everything. And what's really smart is opening yourself to the wisdom of others. That includes mentors, leaders, and experts, but also your management team and your staff.

Sit down with them and truly *listen* to what they have to say. Ask them what's standing in the way of their success and you'll find where your processes break down. Make it safe for them to disagree with you and you'll hear the truth.

Being a great leader means accepting that not everyone will do things the way you would. Accepting that their approach may be the better choice can be hard. It can also save your business.

The same is true for your prospects and customers. Ask them about their experience with your products and with your service, and be humble enough to hear it when improvements are in order. Listen *first*. Listen often.

Be willing to ask for help.

When you're just smart enough, you're also humble. Which means you're willing to admit that you don't know all the answers, and you won't hesitate to seek out advice, help, or guidance. "Ask for help" is one of the most underrated, underused pieces of business advice out there.

And while this should go without saying, once you get some expert advice, you need to be wise enough to follow it. Business owners who are *too* smart seem to have trouble with that.

I've benefitted so much over the years by always being the dumbest person in any room. When you take this position, you'll open yourself up to better ideas. And contrary to what may feel comfortable, there's a benefit to being "dumber" than your employees. When you let them do their own thing, they'll apply what they've learned from the front line (knowledge you may simply not have) and more often than not, they'll rise to the occasion.

Buying a business can sometimes be easier than starting one.

It takes time to generate revenue from a business. Which means that at start-up, you'll need cash flow. When you buy an existing business, revenue streams are already in place, which means cash is already flowing. It also means that the owner before you paid the "beginner's tax" when they made their own mistakes in learning how to generate that revenue. That's a savings for you in dollars, time, and energy.

And don't underestimate the value of training from the former owner. I recommend working with them for at least a year. Because the truth is, you don't know what you don't know. And the person who ran the business before you will show you that. It's also unrealistic to assume you'll do better than the previous owner in Year

One. It's only natural that things will come up and mistakes will be made. So account for the learning that's to come.

If you're buying a franchise, follow the plan.

The most critical advice I give franchise buyers is to follow the business plan provided by the franchisor. Time and again I've watched business owners buy franchises and then modify the plans. They think they know better. They get too smart. And then their businesses fail.

Trust me when I tell you that franchisors have invested tremendous amounts of time and money in establishing plans that work. If there were a better way, they'd use it, because they'd be able to charge higher franchise fees. Follow the business plan and you'll have a much, much better chance of creating the life you want to live.

Set up an advisory board.

Every business should have an advisory board. This isn't the same thing as a board of directors, which has oversight and legal responsibilities. An advisory board is a group that convenes to give you support, advice, insights, and guidance. You'll be wise to tap people within your own network who have pertinent experience or expertise. People who will be pulling for you.

That said, you'll be even wiser to also choose some naysayers and doubters. You want your advisory board members to spot potential roadblocks or pitfalls. And you want them to be honest with you—sometimes brutally honest—as those things arise.

You also need to choose people who are out in front of you. If they've traveled the path before, they'll be much better suited to guide you down it. And while family members may be enticing candidates, they aren't always comfortable giving critical feedback or uncomfortable advice, and we may be more sensitive to hearing it from them than from outsiders we consider to be experts.

Your advisory board should be on the smaller side—three to five people or so—and will meet just a few times each year. And while members of advisory boards don't get paid, it's nice to recognize them with perks like travel or meals or gifts, and take care of them like family.

Read voraciously.

If you're not keeping up with the business books on the best-seller list, now is a great time to start. Being too smart means reinventing the wheel because you assume you already know it all. Being just smart enough means reading about how the wheel was invented and following the diagram in the book (and these days, the YouTube videos and podcast that accompany it). I've learned almost as much from business books as I have from running my own business. Beyond that, read books about human behavior and psychology, history and economics, and skill sets for leaders such as sales, persuasion, communications, and negotiation.

Network in your industry and join peer groups.

Every major industry has a network of competitors, suppliers, journalists, trade associations, and lobbying firms. If you're just smart enough, you'll get involved in the alliances that have formed inside yours. Find peer groups and join them. Seek out best practices and industry standards, and compare your progress. Get to know the competition inside and out. And build a group of colleagues you trust.

There's an old African proverb that says, "When you want to go fast, go alone. When you want to go far, go together." When you're just smart enough, you realize that business isn't a sprint; it's a marathon. And you're going to need a crew you can trust. Take baby steps with the advice you get, until you're sure that advisor knows what they are doing. Many people have advice to share, but not all of them are people you should follow.

Beyond that, I highly recommend that you give back to the network in the form of expertise, volunteer time, leadership, and money. Be smart enough to realize that you get what you give. And that your role as a leader extends well beyond the people you employ.

Outsource what you don't know.

The outsourcing of subject-matter expertise or operational systems becomes easier and more turn-key with each passing year. You can hire people to complete your hiring or HR functions, handle accounting and bookkeeping, oversee marketing and promotions, and even make sales. And all of the good ones have invested in systems and people who make your life easier and your business more successful.

Outsourcing is especially helpful early on in your business when your expertise may be narrow or your experience limited. As your business grows and evolves, you can bring functions in-house and hire your own teams to implement systems.

Invest in training.

To this day, one of the best investments I ever made was in a comprehensive sales training program for myself. In this program, I learned everything from how to build rapport with a potential client to how to close a sale. I took two weeks out and did a deep dive in a live, on-site program. It made me more confident and agile, and turned me into a much more reliable earner. You'll also need to invest in outside training for your management team and your staff. Lots of people see training as an expense. But it's actually an investment with a real payoff. When your whole operation is properly trained, you'll be more efficient, more effective, and more profitable.

Don't strive for perfection. Strive for improvement.

You're going to make mistakes. Leadership is defined by a never-ending series of learning experiences, and if you're looking for perfection, you'll likely miss the lessons.

The key is not to get everything right the first time, but to learn and improve when you miss the mark.

You may miss sales. You may lose key team members. You may miss opportunities or make decisions that result in wasted money. But with every mistake, the learning curve flattens, and you become better. When you're too smart, you're overly committed to being right. And **being right is never as rewarding as being rich.**

That weekend at the retirement conference, I began to build Team Benetrends in earnest for the first time. I sidestepped my ego and asked for help. I invested in the operational systems we needed to survive and thrive. And in doing so, I set Benetrends up to turn a profit while also operating at scale. That single exercise in humility opened my eyes to a world of possibility.

And I had absolutely no trouble finding my car in the parking that day. In fact, if you read on you'll see why I stopped focusing on my own problems, almost entirely.

Imperative #3:
Focus On Your Clients' Problems And You'll Solve Your Own

If there's one thing you can count on in business, it's that success will ebb and flow. You will be seriously challenged again and again. As I noted earlier, running a business sometimes seems like overcoming a series of obstacles. The degree to which you can move from one to the next while maintaining a positive attitude, true curiosity, and a focus on solutions will determine how likely you are to experience success.

When I returned to the Benetrends office with my newest associate, I cheerfully set out to overcome our present lack of business. I'd dug myself into a hole by being too smart. And I needed a way out.

Thankfully, I still had a relationship with one of my largest pension clients. And he had a problem. He owned a company that designed and produced propulsion control, heating systems, and repair work for ships. He needed capital for his business and was looking for a way to maximize whatever cash he had on hand. My biggest business breakthrough came (as they commonly do) when I stopped struggling to solve my own problems and committed to solving his. I started with what I knew best: I began voraciously studying the tax code.

Somehow I've always had an ability to see things in statutes and laws that didn't seem common. So I used this superpower to find a break in the ERISA. As it turned out, my client was permitted by the tax code to roll over his personal 401(k) funds into the corporation's retirement plan. He could buy shares of his own company using his retirement funds without interest or penalty. He could make use of funds he thought were unavailable to him while making his safest investment yet. He could invest in himself.

Soon I was offering variations of this solution to other clients. First it was a CPA who told me he was buying little bits of his clients' businesses. Next it was a gentleman who wanted to leave his corporate job and buy a hardware store on an island off the coast of Seattle. Then a pottery manufacturer in Orange County. Then a man who'd been laid off and changed jobs five times before he and his wife decided to open an interior design firm.

Each time, I solved a unique problem for one of my clients. I stayed open, curious, and positive. I used the tax code to uncover opportunities, and guided them all into situations where they were empowered, well-funded, and living their dreams. With each new plan I designed, the viability for standardization and mass production improved. I knew I was onto something that could go big.

And then we hit a stroke of luck. One of my clients was interviewed by the *Orange County Register*. They did a two-page spread on my 401(k) rollover plan and how it provided both shelter from the storm of layoffs and a path to prosperity for would-be entrepreneurs. From that serendipitous interview about our unconventional solution, we designed and sold 80 new plans! And a new Benetrends was born.

I'm not going to sugarcoat the facts: In your first few years of business, you will most probably struggle. It may be the most difficult thing you've ever done. I tell every one of my clients that they'll likely lose money in Year One, break even in Year Two if they do everything right, and bring home modest earnings in Year Three if they stay on track. So you'll need a financial cushion to see this process through.

But more than that, you'll need to follow an essential rule if you want to become an essential business:

Solve big problems for your clients, and you'll solve your own problems along the way.

I didn't get my big break because I hired the best salesperson or solved my administration problem. I stumbled upon unprecedented success because I committed myself to the success of my clients.

And I didn't stop with the rollover investment to start their businesses. At Benetrends, we designed benefits plans for these entrepreneurs that allowed them to build real wealth. We helped them give back to their employees, scale their businesses, and create exit strategies that served them in retirement. We stayed with them while they achieved their dreams.

We made Benetrends indispensable to our clients. And it's because we maintain that focus, even today, on solving problems and fulfilling dreams, that we create thousands of new plans each year and provide administration and support for the tens of thousands of retirement plans we maintain.

Following are some tips that will help you solve those big problems for your clients, and in the process, solve your own:

Your client doesn't care about your knowledge.

That may be a hard pill to swallow if you're driven by ego or feeling insecure in a new business. But it's 100% true. What your client cares about are their *results*. They care about how they can save time or money, feel joy, improve their lifestyles, build better relationships, and all kinds of other outcomes your business might provide. They care that you help them meet a goal or solve a meaningful problem in their life. Their interest in your knowledge extends only as far as it affects them personally. So selling them on your knowledge or credentials is futile.

Instead, you should sell them on what their life will be like when you've succeeded on their behalf. And it's there that true innovation and creativity begin and the real effort takes place. Your job is to get them out of the zone they're currently in and into the one where they want to be.

You only get one chance to make a first impression.

In my opinion, leaders and business owners place an inordinate amount of emphasis on closing sales. You'll get lots of opportunities to close a sale once you've built rapport and trust with a potential client. But you'll only get a single chance at an *opening*. And the opening defines the size and scope of your opportunity in every relationship.

If you open the conversation correctly, your prospect will tell you what they desire. They'll tell you their problems and how they have tried to solve them in the past. They'll tell you exactly what they want from you, and how you can convince them to be your client.

But you won't hear any of it if you're working on closing the deal. Because you'll be doing all the talking. A great sales call is 98% what the customer wants and why, and 2% assurance that you can help them achieve it.

When you open with genuine curiosity about your client's problems and goals, you'll create a sincere connection. And that is the first step in building real trust.

You always need to know you did your best.

Being in business is about serving. It's easy to have the impression that once you're the boss, you'll no longer have to serve. But nothing could be further from the truth. When you're the boss, you simply serve *more* people.

As a general rule, you will succeed if you always do your best to solve their problems. Going the extra mile is kind of a cliché, I know. But there's a reason for that: it's the key to success.

Think about a time in your life when you found yourself on the ropes—perhaps what seemed an impossible challenge at work, painful upheaval in a relationship, a health crisis, or a perhaps a financial fallout of some sort. When you find yourself in a fight against an "opponent" who outmatches your capabilities, experience or stamina, there's no better feeling than having someone in your corner fighting for you. When you can share the burden of your problem (or the urgency of your desire) with someone who has your best interests in mind and the curiosity and perseverance to stay with you until the end, you feel fully supported. And you're all in. This is the way your clients should feel.

And it doesn't matter if you're selling them a four-week nutrition plan or a 30-year mortgage. When you fully commit your energy and resources to solving your customers' problems, they'll feel it. And when you make it a priority to always do your best for them, your employees will feel it too. When you create a culture around truly helping people, you create something special. Something enduring. Something you and your team will be proud of: a reputation. And along the way, you'll likely create the kind of revenue and market share your less committed competitors will envy.

Focus on designing relationships, not products and features.

You've likely heard the statistics on the cost of acquiring a new client compared to the cost associated with keeping one. Depending upon your industry, it can cost five to twenty-five times more to bring in a new client that to keep one who's already signed on with you.[6] The bottom line is there's gold in relationships. So everything you design, manufacture, and sell should be geared toward building them. (Not to mention the fact that you'll feel happier and more fulfilled by relationships than transactions.)

When you're developing your products, your processes, your employees, or your systems, the question to ask is, "How can we develop solid, long-term *relationships* with our clients?" When you discover how to be useful—better yet, indispensable—in solving ongoing problems for your clients, you'll build friends for life, and the kind of loyalty that results in referrals, as well.

When life give them lemons, add sugar.

Nobody likes a downer. One of the easiest ways to ingratiate yourself with prospects and customers is to *be positive.* Whether you're grooming dogs or serving lunch, solutions that come with a smile are the ones that bring the surest results. You know how to turn lemons into lemonade? Add sugar!

And the same is true for your clients' problems. Optimism is contagious. When you approach your client's situation with a cheerful "Yes, I will!" you send a clear message about what they can count on from you and your company. You set yourself up for success at the same time you set them up for it.

I can't count the number of people who've asked me over the years, "How are you, Len?" My favorite answer: "If I were any better, you could bottle me and sell me!" Research by the National Center for

Biotechnology Information shows that positivity affects your problem-solving skills. Those who are negative tend to focus on the complexity and severity of the problem, while those who are positive are more open to possibilities, which lead to solutions. People who are positive are more successful because they more easily identify opportunities and are more apt to take advantage of them. They also work better in teams because they bond better and are more open to trusting others. In fact, the act of smiling alone makes it more likely that others will trust you.[7]

During those early days of the entrepreneur rollover plan, we thought if we could do 25 plans a month, we'd live like royalty. Little did we know that someday Benetrends would do hundreds of plans each month. And we would be the catalyst for an industry of competitors who would collectively produce hundreds more. In fact, we helped pull our country out of a great recession once. But I'm getting ahead of myself. First, let's talk about lifestyle. And how it's absolutely everything when it comes to what you're advertising and selling.

Imperative #4:
It's Always About the Lifestyle

If you've bought into the idea that life begins at 50 (and you should, because it's the truth), you'll be delighted to know that I met the love of my life at 60. I'd been divorced for eight years and had built Benetrends into a viable venture when I met Cheryl on Love@AOL, an online dating site. Our first date was at Seaport Village, a tiny little shopping district along the harbor near downtown San Diego. I'll never forget the blue dress she wore. It had little sailboats all over it, and it touched a place in my heart that loves the open water.

I asked if she was hungry. And when she said yes, I replied, "Let's go feed ya." Dinner was a raging success. Nine months later, we were married.

Two days later, we were standing on the deck of a sailboat in the Virgin Islands, preparing to crew a one-week open-sea adventure. Much to our dismay, the boat was filthy and musty. It hadn't been used in ages. And while my intent was to share my love of sailing with Cheryl, and to see how she fared at sea, the execution of my glamorous scheme undoubtedly lacked glamour.

On our first day, we were docked at Salt River Bay on the island of St. Croix, on a magnificent estuary with a lush mangrove forest. I was eager to see Cheryl's reaction to this first little oasis, and I excitedly called her up to the deck to soak in the exotic setting.

"Cheryl, come up here! You have to see this incredible view!"

Cheryl met me up on deck. But she wasn't quite as quick as I was to see the beauty and serenity in our situation. Her attention was immediately drawn to two creatures in the water nearby.

"What's that swimming in the water, Len?" she asked, with more than a bit of trepidation. Within seconds, she was absolutely convinced of the worst. "I think those are sharks! Are we out here with sharks? No one told me there would be sharks!"

Eager to quell her fears (and still convinced I could sell her on my own love of boats), I called for Captain Roger to identify the black animals that appeared to be circling our boat. Being the consummate expert that he was, the captain identified them straightaway.

"Ah," he replied. "Those sea creatures are commonly called snorkelers," he replied dryly. "And they're relatively harmless, overall."

Cheryl's "snorkel fish" were just the icebreaker we needed to laugh out loud and turn that honeymoon into a magnificent sailing experience. Ten years later when we bought our first yacht, we named it *Snorkelfish*.

What I hear from so many entrepreneurs is that they're motivated by the idea of making money. Or that they're interested in building wealth. But the truth is, building a business is hard. Running a business is hard. And one thing I've learned is that it's not the money that keeps people in the game—it's the lifestyle the money will buy.

In those early years of Benetrends' success, Cheryl and I got a taste of a lifestyle we'd never even imagined. And it motivated us to push through the roadblocks that business ownership presented, like the complexities of hiring (and then firing) the wrong people, and the mysteries around whom we could trust in the world of promotions and advertising. It didn't start out as luxurious. But even early on, there were perks that set me on fire.

> **And one thing I've learned is that it's not the money that keeps people in the game—it's the lifestyle the money will buy.**

Not too long after we were married, we moved into a condo in the City Front Terrace in downtown San Diego. We had a balcony, a view, and access to the bustling Gaslamp Quarter and harbor. Around the same time, I moved Benetrends' offices into the One America Plaza building about half a mile away.

Those two decisions elevated my life into a kind of paradise. I'd walk to work in the mornings, meet with clients and their advisors for several hours, and then stroll home to meet Cheryl for lunch. I distinctly remember the absolute freedom and gratitude I felt while walking home to lunch each day, closing sales from my cell phone on the way, breathing in the ocean air, and basking in the Southern California sunshine. It was a dream for me.

Over and over during those years, Cheryl and I returned to Seaport Village, where we'd had our first date and she'd worn that blue dress with the sailboats. We'd spend hours wandering through galleries looking at original art that celebrated the intensity of the ocean and represented the spirit of the life we'd built. We loved the originals by American marine artist and conservationist Robert Wyland, who had painted more than a hundred "whaling walls," and Ferdinand Petrie whose watercolors captivated us. Although I'd never owned an original piece of art in my life, one day I came to the exquisite realization that I could actually afford one...that the lifestyle I had admired and dreamed about was becoming reality.

That evening after dinner, we waltzed straight down to the gallery in Seaport Village and dropped $16,000 on one of the originals we'd been eyeing. It was the most money I'd ever spent on anything other than a house. As they rang up the sale and arranged delivery of the piece, we felt like characters in a movie of someone else's life! And we still chuckle about how we snapped right back into reality when we walked from the gallery to the ice cream shop to celebrate and had to scrounge up pennies to pay for our cones.

About two years later, Cheryl and I bought a house in Coronado with a boat dock attached to our back patio. And before too long, *Snorkelfish* was docked right outside.

We'd dreamed of life by the sea. We'd imagined a home filled with original works of art that celebrated the beauty of our world and showcased the talents of the painters and sculptors we so deeply appreciated. Today, 20 years later, we still live in our dream home on Coronado Island. And we sail on our yacht, *Fischer's Catch*, every chance we get.

I tell you this story not to boast about artwork or boats, but to invite you to get in touch with the lifestyle you want to live. To encourage you to discover what makes you happy and what true financial freedom would look or feel like for you. What would you do with more money than you've ever had before? What would you buy? How would you live if given the chance to create your own dream?

Because it's the lifestyle and not the money that will spur you on when days get tough. And it's the lifestyle that makes entrepreneurship 100% worthwhile. Following are some tips to keep in mind as you design the life of your dreams.

> **Because it's the lifestyle and not the money that will spur you on when days get tough. And it's the lifestyle that makes entrepreneurship 100% worthwhile.**

A salary just isn't enough.

As an employee, your salary is all you can really count on (and as we've already established, sometimes you can't even count on that). But as a business owner, you have access to everything the business can provide—not only income but also benefits that were previously only afforded to your employer. Things like travel, insurance coverage for health and wellness, permissible perks and bonuses, tax-free retirement, deductions for legitimate expenses, vacations, and more.

But very few perks are as valuable than the freedom you'll have when you're running the show. These benefits, when designed according to your needs and administered

properly, can set you up for a pretty phe-
nomenal lifestyle.

You control your destiny.

When you're a business owner, people treat
you differently because you're in control.
You'll no longer be requesting pay increases
from someone who makes decisions about
your income on *their* behalf. You'll move
from asking "Can we afford it?" to "Do we
want to spend money on this?"

Sure, there will be frustrations. But
you have the authority and additional
resources to resolve them. You can choose
who you work with, where you work, what
tasks you complete, and what tasks you
delegate. You decide how you spend your
days, and how you spend your money. My
good friend and Benetrends CEO, Rocco
Fiorentino often says, "When you love
what you do, you'll never work a day in
your life."

Don't buy a business. Buy a lifestyle.

Deciding what kind of business to start
or purchase may be the first opportunity

you've ever had to design a lifestyle that fulfills your own dreams. There's no doubt that revenue and profit will be critical for your success. And I always warn my clients that the first year in any business they will be in survival mode and need capital and cash flow.

But long before you make that first dollar of profit, you'll reap the rewards in terms of your lifestyle. So take time to consider how you want to spend your days and your future. Get crystal clear on what the "good life" means for you, beyond just money.

- Where do you feel hamstrung in your current job?
- What are you missing out on?
- When do you feel most challenged and most alive?
- How would you like to be compensated beyond dollars? In respect? Personal freedom? Enjoyment? The ability to contribute and give back? Self-satisfaction? Creative license?

- If you complete the sentence, "When I open my own business, I'll finally…" what things come to mind?

Don't buy a business—buy the lifestyle you've always dreamed of. Take your time. Do your homework. And design your destiny.

Carefully consider your family connections.

As a new business owner you'll need the emotional and moral support of your spouse, partner, and family. There will be many days that you'll be pushed to your edge. Fighting with your family in addition to fighting through business challenges can produce debilitating levels of stress and self-doubt.

What's more, *starting* a business with your spouse or family members can add a significant number of complications to the process. Relationships are hard enough without the pressure of running an enterprise on top of them. And decisions can quickly become clouded by ulterior motives, expectations, and the desire to avoid uncomfortable conversations. What's more, you can feel obligated to take bad advice, be blinded by love, or feel stuck in situations you'd handle much differently with non-family team members.

Beyond that, every business needs one boss. A single leader. And love relationships (and new businesses) often buckle when one person takes charge. There are times that personal partnerships evolve into wonderful business partnerships (I've been blessed to achieve that in my own business). But by and large, doing business with family is tough. So when you design your lifestyle, be very honest with yourself about what you want to achieve—and what you want to avoid—when it comes to the people you love.

Practice gratitude, and keep wonder alive.

I'm 81 years old, and every day since I started Benetrends I've counted my lucky stars. I never take for granted the amazing opportunities and experiences that business ownership affords me.

> Build gratitude into your day. Revel in your freedom, your power, your choices, your accomplishments. Because the moment you take it all for granted is the moment you'll lose the magic.

Not long after Cheryl and I bought our first piece of artwork, we decided to trade in our little Mazda Miata for something "next-level." Neither of us had ever owned a new car, let alone a luxury one, and we weren't quite sure what to expect when we headed out to the Lexus dealership one Sunday morning. We must not have looked like high rollers, because the salesman steered us toward the least expensive model on the lot. Cheryl and I shared a secret little smile and told him we'd like something a little more well-appointed. A few hours later, we felt like royalty driving off that lot in a gorgeous new Lexus sedan. And we never looked back.

The lifestyle of your dreams may look nothing like mine. But if you're going to weather the storms of business ownership, you'll want to get clear about what success looks like for you. Because it's that vision that will motivate you to leap out of bed each morning, and to stay with it when things get complicated or uncomfortable.

It's been nearly 40 years since I founded Benetrends, and I still have to pinch myself to believe that it's real. It was never about the money. For me, it was always about what the money could buy. That said, in order to fulfill your deepest lifestyle desires, your business will have to compete (sometimes fiercely) with other players in your industry. Read on to see how you can secure your lifestyle by adopting a rare and specific viewpoint on how to compete.

Imperative #5: Make Your Competition Irrelevant

By the time we hit the five-year mark, things at Benetrends were really looking up, and our client portfolio was beginning to grow. Until one of our employees walked out unexpectedly, carrying a whole lot more than he'd walked in with. I won't get into the details of the split other than to say that he intended to take the very things we valued most: our name and our product. And he had leverage to potentially do so. Because we'd been inexperienced in the workings of the internet, we'd allowed him to purchase our company URL—and he'd done so in his own name. As the old saying goes, possession is nine-tenths of the law. And he was in possession of our link to the online world and looking to maximize his advantage.

Before we knew it, we were embroiled in a sticky and uncomfortable lawsuit over both the name of the firm I'd founded and the name of the new retirement plan I'd designed and was delivering to our clients. It felt painfully personal.

When the judgment came through, I got exactly half of what I'd hoped for. We retained ownership of the name Benetrends, but the acronym we'd been using to identify our plans became the property of someone who had officially become "the competition."

You might imagine that lawyers are more experienced with lawsuits and therefore feel less emotional about the process or the outcome of a protracted legal battle. But not in this case. On the day we first reached out to a branding agency to help us rename the product that had become the lifeblood of our firm and the center of our lives, Cheryl and I felt disappointed, angry, and betrayed.

We wondered how we'd begin again when we'd only just begun. We questioned how we could establish ourselves as the originators in the market when someone else was using the name of the process I'd defined and refined.

But more than anything, we felt determined to make our newest competitor entirely irrelevant.

The first step on that fateful morning was about letting go. And if you've ever had someone take something that was yours, you know that's often challenging to do. But as the brand strategist led us through a series of questions and exercises, we came to see the truth.

Up to that point, we'd been playing small. We'd defined the value of our business by our product's features. Bluntly stated, we'd come up with a clumsy acronym to define a retirement plan rollover. And as we released our grasp on the meaningless letters that had felt important enough to fight over only hours before, we opened our minds for the first time to the enormity of our potential.

We did this by first employing Imperative #2 (Be smart, but not too smart) and placing every bit of our attention on the people we intended to serve.

For the most part, our ideal clients were over 40. They'd worked long and hard to establish themselves as managers, leaders, valuable team players, and masters of their skills and trades. And they'd been responsible. Every one of them had saved for retirement and had the 401(k) account to show for it. But they were also burned out. Some had been laid off, others were looking for a way out, and still others had hopped from role to role in the hopes of feeling inspired, challenged, or simply satisfied. Instead, they felt stuck, uninspired, and often powerless.

What we came to realize that morning, and later validated over decades, was that our ideal clients were also letting go.

> They were letting go of fulfilling someone else's dream so they could design their own.

> They were letting go of a lifetime of reliance on someone else's choices and actions so they could step into total autonomy and personal power.

> They were letting go of relying on their employers' business plans for their own prosperity.

> And for the first time in their lives, they were ready to make it rain for themselves.

In the four or five short hours we spent uncovering and naming our clients' hopes and dreams that day, we laid the groundwork for the launch of a brand that would become an industry standard: The Rainmaker Plan®. From that day forward, we would guide our clients to make rain with their rainy day savings.

Unlike our new competitor, we weren't in the financing or funding industry. Our mission was to help experienced, qualified, talented individuals build the kind of lifestyle we'd built for ourselves. The Rainmaker Plan wasn't a financing tool at all. It was a means for competent people to invest in themselves, to build wealth through the design of their own corporate benefits plans, and to grow their own futures.

The Rainmaker Plan is a way for our clients to change the paradigms of their lives. It's a way to go from employee to employer. And because statistics show that business owners are four times more likely to become millionaires than those who work for others[9], this distinction was absolutely critical in making our competition irrelevant—and continuing to do so today.

Our competitors largely focus on the technical aspects of their plans: the rollover of retirement funds and the legal inception of their clients' new businesses. But The Rainmaker Plan adds value year after year. It was designed to help business owners grow wealthy. Inside every plan is a benefits package packed with a punch. Inside every plan is a pathway to a lifestyle that was once a dream.

When the branding consultant arrived that morning, we'd been focused on creating a better name. By the time she had left that afternoon, we'd created something entirely different: a blue ocean strategy.

Make the competition irrelevant.

Making the competition irrelevant means you create a new opportunity to solve client problems, rather than participating in the feeding frenzy of a crowded marketplace. You do what's necessary to differentiate your business from every other, to have prospects and clients see you as a fresh and unique alternative to the solutions they're considering. You create an entirely new opportunity for your client to succeed, in a way that no competitor can replicate.

(You might be thinking this sounds impossible for a small business, but I'll remind you that Cheryl and I were running a skeleton crew from a two-room office when we made our competition irrelevant. And today we're the de facto industry leaders.)

> **Making the competition irrelevant means you create a new opportunity to solve client problems, rather than participating in the feeding frenzy of a crowded marketplace.**

So how can you make your competition irrelevant? Read on for some ideas.

Tell a compelling brand story, and make your customer the hero.

In the story of The Rainmaker Plan, we're not the heroes—we're the guides. Our customers are the heroes. And at the end of the day, they build businesses they love, and retire with real wealth and no regrets. There's nothing in this story about the legal structure of retirement accounts or ERISA (despite the fact that every one of our competitors were talking about these things then and they're still talking about them now).

The story of the Rainmaker Plan is about freedom and opportunity and the beauty of beginning again. It's the hero's journey and how you can become the hero. You don't have to have a big business to have a big story. You just have to make a big commitment to helping your customers fulfill their dreams.

Acknowledge the peril your hero is in.

In every great story, the hero is in peril. And chances are, your clients and customers are too. Whether you sell spray tans or landscaping services, your client likely has real fear and apprehension around the problem they're trying to solve. And they're not only afraid of the problem; they're afraid of your solution. They're afraid they'll choose the wrong provider and lose money or time, that their problem will get worse, that they'll be taken for a ride or experience frustrations or poor service.

So when you address that fear head-on by listening, supporting, encouraging, and creating space and energy for a real conversation, your company will slide naturally into the role of ally or guide. When you acknowledge that what they're going through is scary—when you tell the *truth*—you'll make the competition irrelevant. Because nine times out of ten, your competitors are not only skipping over that conversation; they're doing everything they can to avoid it.

Be something more.

If you're going to make the competition irrelevant, you need to know everything you can about them. Conduct "secret shopper" missions. Study them. Follow their marketing and advertising campaigns. Check their online reviews on Yelp, Amazon, or similar sites. Reverse engineer how they serve their customers by purchasing their products and experiencing their sales, delivery, and follow-up processes. And then be something more.

Competing on price, product features, and benefits is a never-ending game and can often be a "race to the bottom." It's exhausting and, more often than not, ultimately futile. You make the competition irrelevant by creating a customer experience that's *more*.

When clients come to Benetrends, we don't just roll over their retirement funds and create a legal business entity. We engage with their biggest goals. We envision their future. We become part of their long-term business and personal financial strategies. Our clients see us as partners in their success. They rely on us. And we know that in order to maintain those relationships, and our market share, we must take the attitude that we can never be good enough.

Focus on referrals.

There's nothing more valuable than a customer's endorsement. A solid, heartfelt testimonial where your client tells the story of your guidance and their clear result can sway a friend or family member into gladly choosing your firm.

And when you do more and you make your customer the hero, it's natural for them to promote you. You can simply ask if they know anyone who is looking for the same kind of positive outcomes they experienced.

I often hear new salespeople say they are uncomfortable asking for referrals, or that they believe customers will be uncomfortable sharing information about their friends and family members. But the best referrals aren't based on an ask; they're based on a *boast*. You want your clients to brag to their friends about the success they're having (or the dream they're enjoying), and about the role you played. When you create the kind of story people want to tell, you make the competition irrelevant.

Invest in the best people.

I'll provide specific guidance on this later, but the best investment you can make is in the people you hire. After all, the competition can't replicate the work ethic, enthusiasm, charisma, and smarts of amazing team members.

That means you'll need to be a premium employer to attract real talent. And you do that by creating a positive work environment, giving people the chance to succeed, treating your associates like family, and listening to their feedback regarding your products, processes, systems, and internal environment.

Build in a hook.

Getting prospects to sit up and take notice often requires a hook. That's an angle that grabs the potential client's attention, creates interest in your product, and makes them receptive to your marketing messages. It's not the most expensive marketing tactics that win the game; it's the most memorable. You can do this by engaging all their senses—give them something to eat, smell, or listen to.

For the longest time, Cheryl and I sent every new client an unexpected bouquet of exotic Hawaiian flowers. And in this way, we carved out a beautifully fragrant space in their memories, and created conversations about Benetrends for them to have with friends, colleagues, and family members.

The flowers were a hit, but it was the sound of rain that really set Benetrends apart in the early days. We officially launched the Rainmaker Plan when we purchased thousands of rainsticks for a direct mail campaign. If you've never seen a rainstick, it's a hollow tube made from bamboo or cactus filled with tiny pebbles or beans. Small pegs are arranged in a spiral on the inside of the tube, and when the stick is tilted up or down, the beans sliding through the pegs sound just like gentle raindrops falling.

Because we knew that our prospects' trusted consultants would need to understand our services in order to approve and recommend them, we mailed rainsticks to thousands of business brokers, franchisors, accountants, and small-business consultants along with a postcard and brochure introducing the Rainmaker Plan. To this day, it was the most successful campaign we've ever done.

When we called each recipient and introduced ourselves as the ones who'd made it rain in their office, 90% of them said they remembered our package.

And more than half of them gave us a chance to make a presentation.

Through that launch, we opened up an entirely new sales channel. And we established ourselves as both the product originator and the industry gold standard—both positions we hold to this day, 20 years later. But read on to find out how we solidified the market leader position.

Imperative #6: Follow The Money

When I was a kid in New York, Willie Sutton was a famous bank robber. He was born in Brooklyn, and over a 40-year career, he stole more than $2 million while immaculately dressed. He escaped from jail twice. Willie was a character—a wiry little chain-smoking Irishman with a devil-may-care attitude and the respect of the bloodiest organized crime syndicates in America. He was also known as a consummate gentleman, even by the people he robbed! But what he's most known for is a statement he made to a reporter in the mid-1930s.

When asked, "Why do you rob banks?" Willie purportedly replied, "Because that's where the money is."[10]

While it may seem cavalier to take business advice from a bank robber, the guileless genius of Willie's approach has always stayed with me. It became the main driver for The Rainmaker Plan's success in its earliest days. Simply put, day after day, Cheryl and I took those rain sticks and we went where the money was.

Our maxim was even more specific than Willie's. Wherever three or more people were willing to listen, we would go and make a presentation. And while this fundamental rule sometimes led us to everything *but* the money, more often than not, Willie Sutton's advice was a solid tenet for revenue building. It kept us hungry, humble, and truly engaged in the most consequential daily task for any small business. (Not to mention the random discoveries we made along the way. Our mouths still water over the Tex-Mex we discovered in a strip mall during a dust storm in San Antonio following a "speech" where only three very disinterested people had shown up.)

Contrary to what you may think, following the money isn't a broad strategy. The more narrow and precise you are, the more successful your endeavors will be. When you understand in rich and specific detail exactly who benefits most from the results your products or services provide, you can carve out a niche for your business. And it was in those early commitments to go anywhere three or more would gather that we found our first and most profitable market segment.

> **When you understand in rich and specific detail exactly who benefits most from the results your products or services provide, you can carve out a niche for your business.**

Hot on the trail of success, Cheryl and I followed the money to a convention hotel in Pasadena, where a bustling tradeshow for franchisors and business brokers was happening. As it turned out, small business money flowed right through these deal-makers. They had the clients, the know-how, the established systems for leads, and outstanding closing ratios. There was an entire industry in full play. All we needed was a way to insert The Rainmaker Plan into the middle of it.

This particular multi-day event started in the evening. After we'd set up our booth, eaten the standard rubber-chicken dinner and guffawed along with a thousand sales professionals at a comedian telling jokes, we rushed to stand at our table, prepared to tell our story to anyone who would listen.

Instead, we found ourselves utterly confounded as suit after suit strolled right by, without a single connection. We couldn't even make eye contact with any of these gatekeepers and dealmakers. When we went to bed that night we were frustrated. But we were also more convinced than ever that we had indeed found the money. We just needed a solid plan to make it our own.

So over eggs the next morning we hatched one. We decided to take a wild chance with a piece of cardboard and a Sharpie marker. And we could barely contain ourselves as we rushed to our booth before the mayhem of the day began and made a simple and bold assertion in all capital letters, then taped it to a stack of unused brochures on our table as a lean-to:

WE PAY REFERRAL FEES

Lo and behold, it was only seconds before the first franchise broker stopped to shake hands and say hello. By the end of the conference, we'd spoken to hundreds. More importantly, they'd begun speaking—*about us*—to one another. And by Monday, a niche marketing strategy for Benetrends was born.

We took tens of thousands of dollars in business away from that conference. But more importantly, we took away the most valuable lessons of niche marketing. So listen up, because they're super simple to understand, but they require brave, bold action.

Carve out your own little corner of the market.

In every industry, there are major players. For small businesses, competing against them is often futile. Where small-business owners get rich (or eventually become big-business owners) is in owning very narrow, well-defined slices of the market. As they say, in the niches are riches.

Pension planning is an enormous industry. So is small business lending. We didn't set out to compete in either. Instead, we created a solution for a very specific individual: a professional who was leaving the workforce (or had been pushed out) to start their own business, and who had saved at least $50,000 in retirement funds.

When we followed the money to brokers and franchisors, we got even *more* specific.

When you serve a specific niche, you become an expert in their problems. You understand the conversation that's happening inside their heads. You get in touch with their struggles and their dreams. And you can communicate with them intimately and genuinely about what they desire and what stands in their way. The big players can't do this because they have to cast a wider net to reach a bigger audience.

What's more, when you carve out a niche, your advertising dollars are used more efficiently, because you can direct your promotions right at your little corner of the population. Also, your messaging will be more effective because you'll be speaking their language and empathizing with their specific situations.

If you're buying a franchise, the money's in the plan.

I mentioned this earlier but it bears repeating: if you're buying a franchise, follow the plan. In fact, the proven step-by-step strategy is the most valuable element of franchise investment. Franchisors spend big money and tons of time working through the kinks and validating concepts and processes so individual franchise owners don't have to.

In many instances, they'll even provide you with a script that tells you exactly what to say to customers. Don't stray from those talk tracks or from the sales or marketing plans, because they are the only clear route to the money. If you think you're smarter than the franchisor, then don't spend tens of thousands of dollars to invest in their name.

The profit is in people.

No matter what kind of business you're opening, it's people who produce and deliver your products and services, and people who buy them. If you don't like people, you won't like running a business. (And you won't be good at it either.)

Lead with a lead system.

In every business model, you need leads in order to build a reliable, consistent pipeline of sales opportunities. Whether they are obtained in person, online, through third-party channels, or from business-to-business interaction, you need them to make sales.

Before you do anything else, secure your lead source. Determine the daily, weekly, and monthly actions required to generate leads, and build those actions into a system that you or your team members follow religiously. And no matter how busy you get, never take your eye off that lead flow. It's the lifeblood of your business.

Don't bite the hand that feeds you. Fill it.

Leads cost money. It's a reality in business. Don't be stingy with the people who refer customers to you. We've continued to pay the highest referral fees in the business for decades, and it's been worth every dime. But we also understood early on that it wasn't just the money that kept the referrals coming in. It was the fact that we helped business brokers and franchisors close more deals. We're *useful* to them. And we know that issues like the time it takes to get a plan up and running and our ability to make their clients feel at ease through the process are critical. So in the same way you solve problems for your customers, if you have regular referral partners you'll also have to help them solve problems. And they may be different problems altogether.

The weekend we followed the money, Cheryl and I opened up an entirely new delivery channel, just by following the money and solving problems for the dealmakers. And while we'd spent the first evening scratching our heads and kicking ourselves as our prospects strolled right by, the next night I sat with broker after broker explaining how our plans could help them close deals in the moment, and Cheryl sat under a grand piano in an adjacent ballroom—a hand over one ear and a cell phone over the other—calling in Rainmaker Plan applications to the administrators at our office.

So go where the money is. And find a way to take it home with you.

Now…while sales leads are essential, it's also essential that you understand exactly what to sell to those customers. (And I've got a hint for you: it's not your product or service.) Keep reading and you'll see what I mean.

Imperative #7: Nobody Wants To Buy Your Potatoes

Within 10 years of that conference, Cheryl and I had followed the money to become an absolutely formidable market leader. We moved to Philadelphia, where we set up a suitable corporate headquarters in a state that was a little more tax-friendly than California, and where we also had family. A gorgeous suite of offices housed the 80 or so employees we'd hired to sell and service Rainmaker Plans for our growing client base. We'd reached levels of monthly production we'd never dreamed of. In fact, we actually had desks in hallways to accommodate the staff we needed to support our growth!

Cheryl and I were determined to build out the top floor of the building to expand our flourishing operation...until we hit a snag.

One of our main competitors had successfully recruited our sales manager to join their organization. And while we took our eye off the ball to tend to the issues that accompany growth, we began bleeding market share. For the first time since our inception, we were neck-and-neck with another industry player, and our prospects were comparing our products side-by-side.

Each week, we held a sales meeting to train and inspire the diverse group of consultants we'd hired to sell The Rainmaker Plan to business brokers and the general public. It was this segment of our team who first felt the sting of that market-share loss. And they were scrambling to reverse the momentum.

As the tension of competition mounted, I showed up at the sales meeting one morning with an ordinary bag of russet potatoes and tossed it onto the conference room table.

One by one, I asked the consultants in the room to sell me the potatoes in the bag. Initially, we got the kind of presentation you'd expect from a potato salesperson:

First, features: "These potatoes are the best potatoes you'll find on the market today. They are spectacular in terms of size, shape, consistency, and flavor."

Next, we heard about benefits: "The skins of these potatoes are especially rich in potassium, which helps to regulate muscle contractions. The starch provides energy, as well! And when you mix them with milk and butter and mash them, you'll be full and satisfied at a low, low price."

As soon as one of these "old standard" presentations began, I interrupted and asked the next consultant to take a stab at selling me the potatoes. You see, the difference between two bags of potatoes from competing farms (and two retirement plans from competing firms) has nothing to do with features and benefits. In fact, when you place them side-by-side, they are essentially commodities. And the buyer, seeing no discernable difference in the products, will eventually make their choice based on price alone.

I'm not sure how many false starts we had before I called on a salesperson who started his presentation with a question rather than a statement.

"Mr. Fischer," he began, "what do you hope to accomplish with your bag of potatoes? Can you tell me a little about what your dinners are like now, and what a dream meal looks like for you?"

BINGO. We had a winner.

Remember Imperative #3, when you learned about solving your clients' problems and therefore solving your own? The sales presentation is the gateway for this invaluable information and about the results they seek.

No matter what kind of business you open or buy, you'll never really be selling just a product or service—rather, you will always be selling a transformation. You will close sales when you can describe in full detail what your customer will become the moment they're finished preparing the potatoes and they are enjoying the lifestyle those creamy mashed potatoes have helped them create.

No matter what kind of business you open or buy, you'll never really be selling just a product or service—rather, you will always be selling a transformation.

Nobody wants to just buy your potatoes—they want to buy success, whatever their definition of that may be. Your partnership in this success is what will differentiate you from the competition every time.

In my opinion, the ability to sell based on needs is the most important skill for a leader. Therefore it's the number one skill to develop in your team members as well. Without consistent sales, you can't have reliable revenue. And without revenue you can count on, you'll never have the lifestyle that you got into business to create. If you take nothing else away from this book, I hope you'll take this to heart: competing on price sets off a disastrous race to the bottom for your business. And it destroys all the work you've done to make the competition irrelevant.

So if nobody wants to buy your potatoes, how do you ensure that your sales team doesn't try to sell them? Following are some tips to point you in the right direction.

Don't expect perfection.

Selling is a process. If your associates begin by closing one out of every 20 sales, then every "no" represents one-twentieth of the journey to revenue. When you communicate to your team that there's no such thing as failure—only lessons—you'll make it safe for them to try. You'll give them space to develop the confidence, technique, and rapport-building style required to get to your customer's desired transformation and lifestyle.

People are generally uncomfortable with rejection. But "no" doesn't hurt. So encourage your salespeople to get as many no's as possible, and eventually they'll be resilient enough to create that yes.

And the same holds true for you. If you've never sold before, then chances are you'll need real practice. Don't set yourself up for a pass/fail scenario, or failure will be imminent. Instead, take action often and course-correct as you go.

Invest in training for yourself and your team.

Course corrections are tough if you don't have current information. How will you know what to do differently if you don't constantly seek advice? Sales training is probably the single greatest investment I made in myself as a leader. If you'd told me when I was a young, shy, awkward attorney that one day I'd fall in love with the process of selling services and become great at it, I would have laughed at you. But early on I purchased a two-week sales training program from Tom Hopkins. And for decades the lessons I learned in that intensive experience have stayed with me.

If you want to differentiate your business from the competition in a real way, you'll need ongoing training in sales, and so will your team members. Reinvest in training each year. It pays off.

We often bring trainers into Benetrends to keep our team members sharp and to push the edge of their competencies. And we send our associates out for training as well.

Don't skimp on this and don't skip it. Your lifestyle depends on it.

Commit to repetition.

Good sales associates become accustomed to rejection. That's great news, because this resilience allows for persistence and long-term success. But in my experience, it creates a different kind of challenge: once they create a track record for themselves, they'll often reject your advice and guidance.

Salespeople are sometimes superstitious. They're steadfastly committed to their own path and experiences and may be reluctant to try new things—especially new hires who have been successful elsewhere.

Rather than trying to convince them, (you can't sell a salesperson!) provide regular training and role-playing sessions where they can practice. Repeat. Repeat. Repeat. Don't give up. And don't succumb to a litany of sales approaches within your organization. Show your team how you expect them to present and perform, and win them over as they gain traction with your methods. If you're not qualified to lead this charge, find someone who is.

In the interview, ask them to sell you a pencil.

Even after decades in business, I still find hiring to be one of the most difficult aspects of leadership. It's nearly impossible to determine from an interview whether an employee will be a long-term fit. But I've had the most success hiring sales associates when I ask a single question in the interview: "Can you sell me this pencil?" I'm looking for specific traits as the interviewee responds, and you'll likely benefit from looking for them too. Here they are.

Can they think on their feet?

Do they build rapport with you by being empathetic?

Are they creative and comfortable in conversation?

Do they succeed at getting you to like and trust them?

If the interviewee can demonstrate these essential qualities, you may have a winner.

Hire a culturally, ethnically, and experientially diverse team.

Empathy helps create sincere connection and trust. When we can share and understand the feelings and experiences of another person, we can see where they're coming from and understand their goals and the roadblocks that stand in their way.

If you want your customers to truly believe that you care about their feelings, hire a team that represents diverse cultures, ages, genders, and life experiences. Not only will diversity lead to greater satisfaction among team members, a higher degree of innovation, and help create equity, it will also show your prospects that their interests and perspectives are represented in your corporate culture. When you incorporate diverse perspectives, you'll have a much more solid and effective team and create a richer work experience for everyone involved.

Not long after the potato meeting, we hired a new sales manager who understood and celebrated the difference between selling potatoes and developing partnerships for success. Within six months, we'd reversed our downward trend in market share. And within three years, we'd tripled our corporate revenue. We built out that top floor and solidified our position as the market standard.

Meet me in the next chapter for Imperative #8, and learn about when to stand up and fight.

Imperative #8:
Don't Be Afraid To Fight City Hall

While Benetrends was founded on the concept of helping employees become business owners by investing their retirement funds in their own ventures, we expanded over the years to offer a full range of services that help "wantrepreneurs" fund and grow their companies, so we could become true partners in their successes. One of those services was helping clients secure Small Business Association (SBA) loans. We developed relationships with a network of SBA lenders, and Cheryl oversaw a team that became experts in the minutia of the organization's requirements and processes.

While for many of our clients these types of loans were the perfect adjunct to The Rainmaker Plan, they invariably hit a hurdle as we processed their applications: the SBA did not approve of Rainmaker Plan investments as collateral for the loans. And so with every application, our team had to draft a request for an exception and speak with a representative from the agency. By taking the time to demonstrate to the administrators at the agency the position our clients were in, Cheryl's team members rarely received a denial on any of these exception requests. But the process was cumbersome, and it got in the way of Benetrends providing the level of service our clients deserved, especially in the financial climate of real need that arose in 2007, when so many middle managers were laid off and looking for new ways to create independent incomes and wealth.

On average, Benetrends' clients invest about half of their retirement funds in their new companies at start-up. And about 60% of them use some form of supplemental funding to open their new ventures. This means that more often than not these new businesses are well-capitalized and that our clients have savings well beyond what they invest in their own corporations.

In addition, Cheryl was keen to the reality that the new enterprises launched with the help of Benetrends were job creators. And this was critical to the health of our economy during a time when unemployment rates were skyrocketing. Yet day after day, Cheryl and her team presented well-qualified borrowers to the SBA, only to be forced to jump through illogical and time-consuming hoops in order to get them approved.

Until Cheryl decided to push back against the US government.

In early 2008, we traveled with a group of Benetrends managers and a consultant to meet with the Small Business Administration in Washington, D.C. The United States had entered into a full-blown financial crisis by then, and times were tough for many people in our country. Cheryl had seen firsthand how The Rainmaker Plan could give folks a true fresh start—especially people who had planned well and saved for retirement only to be displaced from their corporate careers long before they'd intended to retire.

Our team had done the advance work to get a meeting with the SBA, and Cheryl was our expert on the subject. We had agreed that she would help us frame the issue for the decision-makers in the room. But as we sat awaiting the arrival of the SBA's representatives, I could see that her breathing was becoming more shallow and her eyes were nervously darting around the room while she sat with her hands tightly clasped. She considered herself an operational manager and she was less comfortable than I was with high levels of visibility and being asked to speak out.

It wasn't long before a parade of suits entered the room, and Cheryl found herself face-to-face with Sloan Coleman, a financial analyst for the SBA and a major influencer in the agency's Office of Financial Assistance. It was Mr. Coleman who had to approve the policy overrides to accommodate Benetrends' requests day after day. Cheryl had finally reached a decision-maker directly, and the stakes felt higher than ever.

If you've never been to the nation's capital to meet with government officials or politicians, just know that it can be a wildly intimidating experience. Cheryl was understandably apprehensive about speaking truth to power.

What am I doing here? she asked herself. *I'm not a spokesperson. I'm not a lending expert. Why would anyone listen to me?*

But despite her self-doubt, she did speak up.

"We're just trying to help people open new businesses so they can survive. We're giving options to qualified managers and leaders so they can become self-reliant after their employers let them down, in an economy that's really frightening for them."

As she laid out her case, Cheryl touched on the higher purpose that aligned Benetrends with the SBA. Without fanfare or the need to cajole or persuade, she spoke out loud the hard truths about how rising unemployment was devastating Americans, and about how small business loans could be a saving grace for so many.

We could see from the raised eyebrows and heads nodding that Cheryl's message had landed with Sloan Coleman and with his team. And do you know what happened? They made a deal with her! Cheryl committed to insisting that every Benetrends client applying for an SBA loan invest $1,000 of their personal funds in addition to the retirement funds in their plans. In return, the SBA changed its lending guidelines to permit Rainmaker Plan funds to be used as collateral for their loans.

An individual citizen with no experience in policy-making or lobbying or governmental red tape, Cheryl single-handedly influenced a change in an enormous federal program to accommodate our company's product. All so she could help make our clients' future dreams a reality.

You know why more people don't fight for what they want? Because they're afraid of failure, and it ties them up in knots. The world doesn't say to us, "Here's how you can succeed." Instead it says, "This is the way to avoid a failure." And how do you avoid failure? You stay out of trouble. You fly beneath the radar. You don't make waves. You hold back, stay quiet, and keep out of harm's way.

My advice to you is that when red tape or regulations get in the way of your customers' best interests, go ahead...fight city hall. But remember this: You don't have to be aggressive about it. And you don't have to convince the whole world.

My advice to you is that when red tape or regulations get in the way of your customers' best interests, go ahead...fight city hall. But remember this: You don't have to be aggressive about it. And you don't have to convince the whole world. Just like the old proverb about how to eat an elephant, you can conquer change one bite at a time. Here are some simple ways to do that.

Focus on convincing the individual in front of you.

Every change you seek to implement or barrier you seek to remove involves a series of encounters with individual human beings. And it's much easier to move forward, despite your fear or discomfort, if you set out to change one mind at a time. If you're trying to change a regulation, don't focus on an entire governmental agency. Start with a single person who will hear you out, and who will reap some benefits from the change you seek.

It's easy to catastrophize. It's easy to slide into a victim role or to see yourself in a David versus Goliath situation. And when you do, you'll risk falling into overwhelm, maybe even paralysis. But if you move forward one step at a time, stating your case along the way, you can bring it all down to something you can handle. As anthropologist Margaret Mead said, "Never doubt that a small group of thoughtful, committed citizens can change the world; indeed, it's the only thing that ever has."

Don't do it for yourself...represent the people you serve.

When I was a young pension attorney, I represented my clients in the formation of a special kind of financial vehicle called a VEBA (Voluntary Employees' Beneficiary Association). The IRS had communicated a ruling against VEBAs, and on behalf of my clients I appealed all the way to the national office...and won! I might not have put in the effort, or taken the risk of rejection, for my own well-being. But on behalf of my clients, I was more willing to be brave and resilient.

There's something about advocacy that gives us courage and strength. While we might avoid speaking up for ourselves, we tend to feel emboldened when we work to address the needs of others or to right injustices against those we care about. You'll be more inclined to find your voice if you think it really matters. Rather than fighting, you'll be representing. Rather than persuading, you'll be supporting.

Align yourself with powerful people.

Cheryl got the SBA to allow our programs because she showed them how the decision would help Americans who had been displaced by the economic downturn. She pointed out to them that unemployment rates were rising and the citizens who'd relied on their corporate jobs for stability were the ones experiencing the greatest instability. She was in touch with the everyday struggles Americans needed to overcome. So rather than stating *her* case, she stated *theirs*. And because the SBA was working to solve those exact same problems, Mr. Coleman sat up and listened and was more willing to seek a mutually beneficial solution.

If you want to foster change, find out how you can align with powerful people instead of working in opposition. The key to fighting city hall isn't in fighting at all—it's in finding common ground. Together you'll go further faster.

Don't give in.

As a business owner, you must relentlessly pursue your goals. It's not for the faint of heart. There will be times when you feel outnumbered and outpowered. But giving up is not an option.

The moment you open your new business, you become a leader. It doesn't matter whether you have a single employee or a thousand. It doesn't matter whether you sell sandwiches or insulin pumps. Your work will be important not just to you, but to many people in your orbit. It will require you to put one foot in front of the other every single day. Pushing back against systems, regulations, or decisions that hamper that work won't be easy. But if you don't become comfortable asking for what you want, there's a surefire chance you'll never get it.

Since that day Cheryl spoke up to Sloan Coleman at the SBA—and he really listened—Benetrends has processed thousands of SBA loan applications for budding entrepreneurs. We've developed one of the best loan approval success rates in the industry. As of 2020, we process loans in all 50 states. Benetrends' customers regularly receive loan approvals in less than 48 hours and have access to their funds within a week.

Cheryl's decision to fight city hall has helped create thousands of new businesses and jobs for tens of thousands of people. She had no special powers or experience. No special training or insider knowledge. No big-money backers or powerful connections. Her power was derived solely from her commitment to solve problems for our customers, and her willingness to step through her fear to make a difference.

But fighting city hall isn't the only way to make your business stronger. You'll also need to learn the rules inside and out so you can make the most of any situation. Read on to see what I mean.

Imperative #9:
Learn The Rules So You Can Do What You Want

After we'd struck our cooperative bargain with the SBA, things in the US economy got considerably worse. On the morning of October 1, 2008, it felt like the whole world was on fire. The mortgage and banking industries were in shambles. Lehman Brothers had just collapsed. The government was working on a $70-billion bailout plan for corporations that had previously seemed too big to fail. Unemployment was above 6%, which at the time seemed incredible. Every time you turned on the TV or opened a newspaper, all you saw was financial devastation.

But when I walked into the building on that particular Wednesday morning, our phones were ringing off the hook. Why? Because as Americans had lost their jobs and couldn't find new ones, many of them started looking for ways to become self-reliant. They sought out business brokers and franchisors to explore their options. And the brokers and franchisors sent them to us. So while the whole world was on fire, it was as though Benetrends was surrounded by a moat filled with cool water.

After years of selling, slogging, explaining, educating, and networking, we were finally in a position to simply sit back and receive. We were essentially order takers. And beyond anyone's wildest dreams, we were doing more than 100 new plans each month.

That Wednesday, every consultant in our office was helping a potential new client put out the fire in their own financial life, when the flames of what was becoming the great recession engulfed our industry in a single moment. The spark that jumped across the moat and lit our executive team on fire was an internal memo from higher-ups at the IRS to the agents in the field offices who audited corporate deductions. It was entirely unexpected, 15 pages long, and directed specifically at practices in our industry that the IRS deemed undesirable at best, and at worst made Rollover for Business Start-Up (ROBS) plans illegitimate.

I don't know if you've ever received an unexpected letter from the IRS, but if you're anything like most Americans, you suffer from an enormous innate fear that one is lurking inside every mailbox. (And I'll tell you a little secret: the IRS not only set out to make us afraid, they LOVE it that we are.) Just the mention of their name triggers the same powerful fight-or-flight response as a fire alarm: the sympathetic nervous system jumps into gear and releases hormones that signal the adrenal glands to release adrenaline. Your heart rate, blood pressure, and breathing rates all increase. You feel an overwhelming sense of urgency to DO SOMETHING to save yourself from danger.

Now imagine being privy to a letter from one mucky-muck at the Bureau to another about the entire industry you founded. Think of how you'd feel if you got wind of *15 pages* of reasons the IRS might consider your entire business model invalid…or even dangerous.

So when that memo rolled out of the fax machine at Benetrends, our team flew into an absolute panic. The phones were still ringing, but nobody knew whether to answer them or not.

I walked in that morning to find our COO barking out orders, sweating, and gaming out worst-case scenarios. I stood, totally bemused as the experts we'd hired to manage compliance, sales, and administration talked over one another, paced the office floor, and waved the letter around as they described one terrifying scenario after another.

The fire alarm was so loud and so shrill inside our industry that morning that our largest competitor actually shut their doors. Their attorneys told them it simply wasn't safe to do business.

But as our own team was falling to pieces, I was giving high fives. As some of our managers lost control of themselves, I experienced both profound serenity and absolute vindication. Because I knew the truth: The IRS letter wasn't a danger to us at all. In fact, for Benetrends, it was the hook-and-ladder that had arrived to save us.

You see, before that day, the biggest fight I'd had in selling Rainmaker Plans was with people who said, "You can't do this. It's against the law." Even other pension attorneys had doubted the legality of The Rainmaker Plan. But I knew all along it wasn't against the law. In fact, the plans were created *using* the law. And while the IRS is perceived as an impediment by almost every business owner out there, the truth is that written tax law is an absolute haven for things you *can* do…if you only open your eyes.

When I read those 15 pages carefully, I saw that the memo laid out in meticulous detail every single thing that rankled IRS auditors about our competitors' plans, but not ours. Once that document hit my desk, I was even more resolved to move forward and scale our business, because I could prove that we consistently complied with every regulation and concern they addressed. I knew our plans were totally clean. I wasn't afraid; I was emboldened.

And do you know what? That letter led to the biggest sales month in Benetrends' history! When our largest competitor shut their doors, their clients came to us. A week later when we showed up at a trade show, their booth sat completely empty, save for a bare white folding table and two empty chairs. We wrote so many plans for business brokers that weekend, we couldn't wind down the energy, even after we'd gone to bed. We were on fire, but in a wonderful way.

Out of the circumstances that drove an entire industry into an overreactive stress response, we became the de facto industry leader—and we still hold that position today. In the wake of that letter, Benetrends set the standard for plan requirements, setup, and administration. We captured an even bigger chunk of market share than we had before.

And we stepped into that leadership role in a very deliberate way: by hiring a lobbying firm and heading to Washington, D.C. to meet the IRS head-on. I wasn't going to stop until I heard them say, out loud and without reservation, that our plans were absolutely permitted by law.

We left for D.C. armed with well-documented facts we intended to use to save the industry. First, we knew our plans were written to the letter of the law. And second, we'd seen studies commissioned by franchise industry experts that showed just how many jobs our plans had helped create. In a climate defined by financial strife, we were offering real solutions that rippled through the market.

The lobbying firm we'd hired knew their way around D.C. They took us to meet with congressional staff members, our representative Allison Schwartz, and members of the House Ways and Means Committee. Cheryl and I strolled straight through the halls of Congress and into a meeting with some bigwigs from the Treasury Department. We were in awe of how far we'd come.

The group who saw us that day were unofficially called the Vice Squad, because it was their job to find weakness or corruption in whatever corporations were doing. So I needed to make sure there were no flaws whatsoever in our business model or our products.

There were 17 competitors in the ROBS industry at the time, all offering 401(k) rollover plans for business start-ups. But our plans were different, because they were written *specifically* with tax law in mind. They weren't about start-up at all; they were about entrepreneurship.

Not only were our plans used to fund new businesses, we also had ongoing relationships with our clients who used the plans to secure their futures, build wealth, and benefit their employees. While our competitors were building businesses selling start-up transactions, we were helping thousands of small businesses to thrive year after year. We had never received an unfavorable IRS opinion letter about a single plan we'd created. And I made sure that the Vice Squad knew we weren't playing games, and that I was prepared to set an example, and even to play a role in policing the industry if need be.

After I told them about our commitment to creating jobs and to serving our clients with real relationships that solved real problems, I told them that I feared they'd dismantle an industry that was moving people forward. I was worried that they'd shut the plans down simply because they didn't like them…that they'd pick wings off of a fly, so to speak, because they could.

But they responded, "Len, we're not here to put Benetrends out of business." What's more, they told me that I'd been right all along! That there was nothing illegal about our plans. In fact, by the end of the meeting, they actually thanked me and said they appreciated where I was coming from.

Imagine…an ordinary pension attorney like me, armed with nothing but a degree from the Brooklyn Law School and the curiosity to wander down a rabbit hole inside the ERISA to help my clients, confronting officers at the highest levels of the US Treasury Department and walking away with their support.

People have asked me many times since that day how I remained confident about The Rainmaker Plan's legitimacy, even as it had been questioned ceaselessly for more than 20 years by accountants, business managers, tax preparers, and even my own management team. My response to them is simple: I had a clear understanding of what we were *permitted* to do. I never once focused on what we were *forbidden* from doing. I had no desire to define our limitations. All of my energy and effort had always been spent on unearthing possibilities.

If you want to create innovative solutions and experiences for your customers and become the brand standard for your industry or market, you'll be wise to take this reality to heart: **The quality of our outcomes in any given endeavor is directly related to the quality of the questions we ask along the way.**

The quality of our outcomes in any given endeavor is directly related to the quality of the questions we ask along the way.

So don't ask what's prohibited; ask what's allowed. When you do, opportunities will present themselves at every turn.

As an attorney, I was trained to think this way. As an entrepreneur, that training has become my single greatest weapon. Here's how you can use this secret weapon to your own advantage:

Know the rules.

If you're going to play any game to win, you need to know the rules inside and out. Read the manual, my friend. Do your research. Due diligence isn't just about staying out of trouble; it's about setting yourself up for massive success. Become an expert in the regulations, guidelines, laws, and agreements that govern your business.

You don't need to break the rules to be successful; you must simply use them to your advantage. There's something to be said for following your gut. But when you back up the intuition with data, you'll be operating at a whole different level. And you'll be thinking differently than 99% of your competitors.

Stay curious.

Curiosity may have killed the cat, but it made the small business owner rich. I often find our clients to be very fixed in their thinking. They have rigid expectations regarding how things will go. And much of this stems from working inside organizations that prize systems and reward those who follow them.

You'll find it's much more profitable over the long haul to be rigid about your expectations in terms of results, but curious about how you'll achieve them. Consider your business journey like a summer-long car trip. You can be 100% fixed about your destinations while remaining entirely open-minded and inquisitive about the various routes to get there. In fact, it's fun to imagine them and play through scenarios.

Asking "How can we…?" is an unconventional and clever approach to business, yet it's the natural basis for all of our childhood experiences. As children, we approached the world with wonder and awe. We tinkered and tested and asked questions until our parents and teachers rolled their eyes at us. If you approach your business with that same level of openness and curiosity, you'll discover new ways on a regular basis, and you'll encourage innovation within your team.

Resist the urge to play Chicken Little, and discourage it in your organization.

I can't tell you how many times the managers in my organization have told me the sky is falling while I'm feeling inspired by opportunity. Once you turn to Chicken Little thinking, you cut yourself off from possibilities. If you believe that problems are threatening, or that having them is a sign of weakness or failure within your organization, you won't have the mental capacity to solve them.

There's a benefit in every problem you solve. Every time you discover a new approach, work around an obstacle, eliminate a snag, or overcome a complexity that feels insurmountable, you build resilience in your organization and you expand your capacity for success.

Giving up Chicken Little thinking is simple if you develop a three-step habit around problem solving:

1. Define the situation.
2. Define what you would like the situation to be.
3. Uncover the obstacle that's keeping you from your desired situation.

Once you've defined the facts, you can begin brainstorming specific, actionable solutions to overcoming the obstacle that's in your way.

But when you panic or fall into a constant state of worry, you focus all of your energy and effort on the problem and none on the solution. Worry and panic eliminate your ability to be present in the current situation, because they throw you into either an imagined future or a remembered past. They eliminate your ability to be creative, responsive, and innovative.

We need "white space" to solve problems and generate ideas. But if your head is filled with dark thoughts and swirling predictions of doom, you'll never find the space you need to get to real solutions, and you'll shut down others who are trying to do so.

Hire advisors from smaller firms.

As your business grows and develops, you'll need advisors along the way: accountants, tax preparers, attorneys, management consultants, HR firms, and the like. Over many decades running businesses and helping others to open them, I've found that larger firms generally squelch creativity.

When you hire professional service providers from big firms, they use cookie-cutter approaches and focus on keeping you out of trouble rather than developing creative ideas about how you can succeed. Advisors with an entrepreneurial spirit and solutions-oriented logic will be your best bet. You want advisors with the same degree of curiosity and can-do attitude that you're working to develop. People who will work around roadblocks, not throw them in front of you.

When I was a kid, I devoured science fiction novels. Sometimes I read three or four in a day! I loved the stories' imagination and creativity, letting my mind flow free to consider the possibilities that the writer had laid out before me—a world entirely without limitations or judgment.

The *Dune* series by Frank Herbert was my absolute favorite. And while my law degree and my deep knowledge of ERISA led me to develop The Rainmaker Plan, my love of science fiction allowed me to imagine creative solutions for my clients that most others wouldn't even consider.

It tickles me to know that all those nights spent under the covers with a flashlight and a paperback gave me the ingenuity and inspiration to create an entire industry, in spite of the skepticism and nay-saying of virtually everyone I met along the way.

We're almost to my last imperative for business success now...and it just may be the most important one. So stick with me!

Imperative #10:
Hire the Best, Overpay, and Encourage Them To Disagree

Some years ago, we hired a consultant named Steve who'd been extremely successful in the franchise industry. His desk was just outside my office, and I often heard him conversing with clients and practicing his rapport-building and sales pitches. One day, I heard him speaking to a potential new client on the phone. He was eager, empathetic, polite, and committed to the client's success. But he was also delivering information that was patently incorrect.

I got up from my desk, walked out to his, and said, "Hang up the phone, please."

Steve's mouth dropped open and he leaned back in his chair, eyes wide. But he continued talking to the customer.

"I said hang up."

His brows knit and he shook his head, indicating how confused he was by my request, so I reached over and pushed the button to terminate the call. Our new associate was speechless.

I said, "Put your headset down, grab a notepad and some paper and that caller's phone number, then come into my office, please."

He did exactly as he was told, and by the time his bottom hit the seat, I could see that he was breathless, and beginning to break a sweat.

As Steve looked on, I called the customer back. "Hello, Mr. Smith?" I inquired. "My name is Leonard Fischer and I am the founder of Benetrends and an ERISA attorney. I overheard our new consultant speaking with you about your new business. I know he's well-meaning and eager to help you. He was also giving you some incorrect information that could get you into trouble, so I wanted to call you myself and prevent any misunderstanding. He's not being reprimanded. He's here with me now, taking notes and learning as he goes."

After the call, this new associate and I had a conversation about truthful communication, candid feedback, and the safety to grow through making mistakes. I assured him that I hadn't meant to scare him, but that it was critical for me to interrupt the flow of misinformation. I asked him if he had questions and if he understood where the call had gone wrong and what to do differently in the future. I made sure he understood that he could always ask for guidance and support, and it was okay to admit when he didn't know something. He could look to me or another team member for clarity. He thanked me. And we even had a laugh about how nervous he'd been in the moment.

Shortly thereafter, that prospect became a client, and our new consultant had his first complicated deal on the books.

Steve eventually became our Vice President of Business Development. Over the course of a decade, I called him into my office many times—not only to give him feedback but also to ask him for advice. As with all of Benetrends' associates and advisors, I encouraged him to tell the truth about what he saw, what he thought, and what he believed to be the best course of action for our company in myriad situations—even when he disagreed with me. When he would hesitate, I'd pull it out of him.

"Just say it," I urged. "Nothing's going to happen. Keep talking—I want to know what you think."

These principles of working hard for the customer, telling the truth, asking for support, and speaking your mind are the main tenets I've communicated to employees for years. And if you employ those same principles, you'll create real relationships with high performers, and they'll stick around to grow and transform your organization. If you can make it safe for your associates to give and receive feedback, you will have nailed one of the most complex aspects of running a business.

Products don't make businesses successful; people do. And if you're going to lead the market, you'll need the best people. You'll need to attract, hire, challenge, reward, and maintain them.

Products don't make businesses successful; people do. And if you're going to lead the market, you'll need the best people. You'll need to attract, hire, challenge, reward, and maintain them.

I've always had a simple philosophy around building a team: hire the best people, pay them more than they're worth, make it safe for them to grow and speak their minds, and treat them like family. For more than four decades, those principles have served me well, along with a few others I learned along the way.

Don't surround yourself with yes people.

Good people have opinions. They have knowledge, experience, skills, perspectives, and ideas. And they want to put them to use. That's what makes them good people!

If you're going to make the competition irrelevant, you won't be able to do it alone. You'll need a team of talented superstars you can count on, because it's impossible for you to know and be good at everything. That means there won't be any room for your fragile ego or burning need to be right.

In fact, in many cases the best course of action will be to admit that you *don't* know the best course of action, and to look to your team members for input and even argument. I've always had an office with an open door and an open invitation for debate, pushback, and differing points of view. And I've never demanded that team members get it right the first time—only that they're committed to getting it right.

Passion is more effective than pressure.

If you asked any long-term Benetrends associate, I suspect they'd tell you they learn something new nearly every day at work. Over 40 years, we've ventured into countless new areas of expansion and discovery. I've never pressured my team. Instead I've encouraged them to join me in the fun! And I've shared with them my passion for the people, the products, and the endless puzzles of running a complex business.

People tend to give more when they're offered understanding and encouragement. They participate more when they're invited into the process. They innovate more when they're encouraged to take action, even when it's imperfect. Contrary to what you may have been told, good business is most definitely personal. And good relationships are built on trust, common understandings, shared interests, and vulnerable moments. Pressure rarely solves problems. But passion? It's at the heart of nearly every truly inspired solution.

Business is personal, but don't take it personally.

This is tricky but it's critical. You'll need to invest time, energy, money, and emotion into the people who work for you. And you'll do well to learn not to take their actions, decisions, or commitment levels personally. It's never about you; it's always about solving problems for the customer, which is the end-result of an effective team dynamic. You'll need to give your team members love and support, but you shouldn't expect to *get* love and support from them. You may have to get that somewhere else.

Likewise, you'll need to be able to respectfully disagree about process, systems, and day-to-day decisions without taking things personally. As an attorney, I learned early in life that I could argue vehemently with brilliant colleagues and then have drinks with them after work. Your work will *be* personal, but you can't take it personally.

Be willing to let people go.

Ask any successful business owner or CEO and they'll tell you that terminating associates is the worst part of running a business.

Hiring isn't a science; it's an art. Sure, there are tests and tools and data that will make the process more exacting. But you will never bat a thousand, which means you'll likely have to let some people go for poor performance, unreliability, or any number of other issues.

It's uncomfortable. It feels awful in the moment. But it's absolutely necessary—for the business and for the associate. Every moment that you keep an employee who's not cut out for the job, you'll jeopardize the success of your team and your business.

But here's the part that some people miss: you also put the employee in a horrible position by keeping them around. No one wants to fail at a job day after day. It's a soul-crushing experience.

So follow the oldest adage in the book: hire slow, but fire fast. As soon as you know that an employee is ill-placed in the organization, help them move on. If you are unwilling to do this, find a manager who is. If you insist on hanging on to employees who can't do the job, you'll be making the choice to let go of your business investment.

Being generous isn't altruistic…it's good business sense.

We established early on in this book that you're going into business for *yourself*. You're making this move to satisfy your craving for a different lifestyle than the one you have now. But once you've satisfied those cravings, you need to give back generously to your team members.

If altruism isn't your thing, I can assure you there's a strong business case for generosity. Good people won't last long if they're not well compensated. They'll need money, attention, recognition, a chance for advancement, and an environment that allows them to thrive. And you'll need good people in order to make the competition irrelevant. Investment in their fulfillment is a direct investment in your own.

Make it a family affair.

I know it may not work for everyone, but Cheryl and I have always benefitted from making our employees feel like family. We've hosted barbecues and parties, hired ice cream trucks, and organized team trips to Broadway plays. We've dressed up like Bonnie and Clyde for the office Halloween party, taken part in countless office pranks, and made more early morning bagel deliveries than we can even remember.

Get to know your employees. Shake their hands, know their worlds, connect with them in real ways. Remember when I mentioned how big corporations broke the social contract? As a small business owner, you have an opportunity to right that wrong. Beyond money, healthcare, and a retirement plan, employees benefit when you provide a positive social atmosphere. (And it will be a lot more fun for you too!)

While I don't recommend making your family members employees, I do recommend treating your employees like family.

Resist the urge to micromanage.

Your business is your baby. I get it. But running it well will mean letting the people you hire do their jobs. If you hire the best, you should feel comfortable giving them the freedom they need to succeed. Be there for support and feedback, but trust your gut enough to rely on the experts you invested in.

When you find yourself being overly pre-scriptive about the process (rather than the outcome), you'll know you're microman-aging. If you make it safe for your team members to come to you with questions and challenges, you can be sure you'll hear about it if they're unable to achieve the goals you've set for them. But if you step in too early or too often, you'll squelch inno-vation and passion, and you'll send your high performers running for the hills.

I'd be doing you a real disservice if I didn't share with you the most painful lesson Cheryl and I learned about running a business: at some point, if you do it well, it will outgrow you, and you'll need to step aside.

At the suggestion of our management team, we'd hired a consulting firm to assist us with growing pains inside the organization. We'd taken on a big new slice of market share after the IRS issued the ROBS memo, and we were all being called to manage workflows and workloads like we'd never seen before. Cheryl and I had both entered the consulting engagement with open minds, and we'd anticipated coming out of the week with new skills and perspectives that would allow us to lead more effectively and reduce the everyday friction that was slowing the organization's progress. Imagine our surprise when we realized that *we* were the very source of the bottleneck.

With each leadership exercise we engaged in, it became painfully clear that our managers would be more effective if we stepped back and allowed them to take over the daily operations of Benetrends. We had outlived our usefulness inside the management team. Yet we were unsure how to process this new understanding, because we hadn't lost our lust for the hustle and bustle of the office, the camaraderie of the team, and the problem-solving that kept our brains active and engaged.

On the third or fourth day of the consultant's visit, he showed up with crowns for the two of us. He proclaimed Cheryl the queen and me the king of Benetrends. And for the remainder of the week, we came to grips with our new roles: to provide oversight, stability, and resources for our leaders, and to participate in high-level strategy. By the time the consultant had left, we knew we'd have to leave right behind him, and start a new era of our lives.

For more than 40 years, every time I talked with a client about starting a new business, I asked them how they planned to leave it. After all, The Rainmaker Plan was created to help business owners build wealth and live the lifestyle of their dreams, right through their final days. I felt so proud that we'd built an organization that could thrive without us—that Benetrends had spawned an entire ROBS industry that launched tens of thousands of businesses with hundreds of thousands of employees.

In the years since I gave up my role as CEO and assumed a position as trusted advisor, Cheryl and I have lived a life by the sea beyond our wildest imaginations. We've found purpose in an entirely new level of contribution to our families and society. We've found joy in one another and in the bountiful fruits of our labor.

So hire the best. Pay them more than they're worth. Give them space to work their magic. And invite them to speak their truth. And you'll build an organization that may outgrow your abilities but will forever bankroll your dreams.

CONCLUSION:
Your
Invitation

t's time to ask yourself that question I mentioned at the beginning.

Who would you rather rely on to secure your future? You or your employer?

If you've stuck with me this far, I'm guessing you're committed to creating your own business to support the lifestyle of your dreams. You may also feel like you've been drinking from a firehose! Or you may feel afraid or unsure of yourself. That's totally natural. Every new business owner feels some degree of fear. If you weren't afraid, it would mean you're not taking it seriously!

If you're ready to begin this wild and wonderful journey of entrepreneurship, I recommend following three steps:

1. Do your research to find the perfect business to suit your skills and your lifestyle. Don't rush in making this choice. Talk to lots of

people. Ask endless questions. Get to know your chosen industry inside and out.

2. Work with a business broker to negotiate whether you're going to purchase an existing business or a franchise. Brokers are well-versed in the transfer of ownership, and they'll work on your behalf to get you a fair deal and alert you to any red flags along the way.

3. Contact Benetrends before you begin!

If you're anything like the thousands of professionals we've helped to set out on their own, then you're ready to begin your dream of opening a business, but you may be hesitant to take out a small business loan that you have to pay interest on. Fortunately, there's an alternative. You have the option to use your 401(k) to start a business, without paying upfront taxes or early withdrawal penalties.

You have the option to use your 401(k) to start a business, without paying upfront taxes or early withdrawal penalties.

As you know by now, The Rainmaker Plan was pioneered by yours truly at Benetrends Financial in 1983. It has helped thousands of entrepreneurs like you receive funding in a manner that is safe, effective, and legal. It's also quick—many receive their funding in as few as 10 business days.

With The Rainmaker Plan, you're able to grow and succeed in business quickly. What's more, the absence of debt and monthly payments means you're also poised to thrive over the long term. You still need to pay your bills and living expenses while you are starting out. That's why our plan enables you to take a salary once you form an active business.

And you won't be alone, even after you receive funding. At Benetrends, we partner with you, rooting for your success for as long as you need us. Here are just a few of the ways you receive the best service in the industry from Benetrends:

- In-house team of certified professionals; no subcontractors or outsourcing of retirement plan services
- Custom plan designed specifically for you, including 401(k) and profit-sharing options

- More experience than any other provider, and a knowledgeable team of experts with the most industry certifications
- Audit Shield protection
- Assurance in knowing that we've NEVER had a plan disqualified!

While The Rainmaker Plan is our flagship product, we also offer a comprehensive suite of funding vehicles that can be used individually or in conjunction with Rainmaker. To find the berst solution, one that is absolutely right for your business and its growth, Benetrends Financial helps you customize a funding option that best meets your current and future needs—a service that other funding companies don't provide. These offerings include:

- SBA loans (97%+ loan approval success rate),
- Securities-backed lines of credit,
- Equipment leasing,
- And conventional business loans.

At Benetrends, we know that business isn't just about the money you make—it's also about the money you keep! So we created the Rainmaker Advantage Plan® to help you build wealth and mitigate taxes. It's a capitalization structure, designed around an exit strategy that allows you to dramatically reduce or eliminate taxes on the profits from the sale of the company.

Of all the things to consider when opening a small business or franchise, you might think the least important would be an exit strategy. But the best time to think about the end game is when your business is just beginning. When the lifecycle of a business ends, an owner's goal isn't about the money that's already been made, but the wealth that will be available after the company has been sold.

That's why it's critical to understand tax implications well before you decide to sell. The way your company is structured in the beginning will set the tone for the life of the business, so you must carefully consider the best options for your company. By planning ahead (like Cheryl and I did), you will be able to enjoy your golden years knowing you have prepared for a retirement that is cash-rich and tax-free!

I hope you've enjoyed spending these hours with me. And that you'll discover riches and pleasures untold by following my Ten Imperatives For Business Success:

#1: Don't Be Afraid To Start In The Middle

#2: Be Smart…But Not Too Smart

#3: Focus On Your Clients' Problems And You'll Solve Your Own

#4: It's Always About The Lifestyle

#5: Make Your Competition Irrelevant

#6: Follow The Money

#7: Nobody Wants To Buy Your Potatoes

#8: Don't Be Afraid To Fight City Hall

#9: Learn The Rules So You Can Do What You Want

#10: Hire The Best, Pay Too Much, And Encourage Them To Disagree

I'm tremendously grateful for the opportunities business ownership has afforded me, and I'm thrilled at the prospect of you enjoying the same kind of freedom, wealth, and joy that I've been fortunate enough to experience.

The road will not be easy. But the rewards are unimaginable.

To your success,
Len

Many thanks to Rocco Fiorentino, who kept after me to write this book. And to Julia Hook.

End Notes

1. Lowenstein, Roger. "The Long, Sorry Tale of Pension Promises." *The Wall Street Journal*, Dow Jones & Company, 1 Oct. 2013, www.wsj.com/articles/SB10 001424127887323308504579085220604114220.

2. Bond, Tyler. "What Happened to Private Sector Pensions?" National Public Pension Coalition, August, 2016,

3. https://protectpensions.org/2016/08/04/happened-private-sector-pensions.

4. "How many American workers participate in workplace retirement plans?" Pension Rights Center, 15 July, 2019, http://www.pensionrights.org/publications/statistic/how-many-american-workers-participate-workplace-retirement-plans.

5. "What States Are At-Will?" Rocket Lawyer, 2021,

6. https://www.rocketlawyer.com/business-and-contracts/employers-and-hr/recruiting-and-hiring/legal-guide/what-states-are-at-will-employment-states.

7. Danko, William and Stanley, Thomas. *The Million-aire Next Door.* Taylor Trade Publishing, 2010.

8. Adlai Stevenson I Quotes. (n.d.). BrainyQuote.com. Retrieved June 8, 2021, https://www.brainyquote.com/quotes/adlai_stevenson_i_155710.

9. Gallo, Amy. "The Value of Keeping the Right Customers." *Harvard Business Review.* October, 2014,

10. https://hbr.org/2014/10/the-value-of-keeping-the-right-customers.

11. Holden, Kristie. "Six Ways Positivity Can Increase Productivity." Market Circle, 25 April, 2016,

12. https://www.marketcircle.com/blog/6-ways-positive-thinking-can-increase-productivity2.

13. Danko, William and Stanley, Thomas. *The Million-aire Next Door.* Taylor Trade Publishing, 2010.

14. "Famous Cases and Criminals: Willie Sutton." Federal Bureau of Investigation, retrieved 8 June, 2021, https://www.fbi.gov/history/famous-cases/willie-sutton.

About the Author

LEONARD FISCHER is a pension attorney specializing in the Employee Retirement Income Security Act of 1974 (ERISA) and the founder of Benetrends Financial. In the 1980's, he invented The Rainmaker Plan™, an innovative financial solution that allows wantrepreneurs to use their IRA and 401K funds to start and capitalize their own businesses without upfront taxes or early withdrawal penalties. Despite the fact that Len has helped tens of thousands of Americans *Make It Rain*, he lives on the sunny side of life, fueled by unrelenting optimism, persistent curiosity, and a mind that naturally looks for a "better way" in virtually any situation.

He was born in Brooklyn and attended the Bernard M. Baruch College in New York City and the Brooklyn School of Law. An entrepreneur by nature, Len is a father, grandfather, avid sailor, and art collector. He lives on Coronado Island with his wife, Cheryl.

Made in the USA
Las Vegas, NV
23 August 2022

53853419R00095